Colin's Campus

Colin's Campus

Cambridge Life
and the English Eclogue

Gary M. Bouchard

SUP

Selinsgrove: Susquehanna University Press
London: Associated University Presses

Associated University Presses
440 Forsgate Drive
Cranbury, NJ 08512

Associated University Presses
16 Barter Street
London WC1A 2AH, England

Associated University Presses
P.O. Box 338, Port Credit
Mississauga, Ontario
Canada L5G 4L8

The paper used in this publication meets the requirements of the American National Standard for Permanence of Paper for Printed Library Materials Z39.48-1984.

Library of Congress Cataloging-in-Publication Data

Bouchard, Gary M., 1961–
    Colin's campus: Cambridge life and the English eclogue / Gary M. Bouchard.
        p.   cm.
    Includes bibliographical references (p.) and index.
    ISBN 1-57591-044-6 (alk. paper)
    1. Pastoral poetry, English—History and criticism.   2. English poetry—Early modern, 1500–1700—History and criticism.   3. Spenser, Edmund, 1552?–1599—Homes and haunts—England—Cambridge.   4. Spenser, Edmund, 1552?–1599—Knowledge—Cambridge (England)   5. Spenser,   Edmund, 1552?–1599. Shepheardes calender.   6. Fletcher, Phineas,   1582–1650. Piscatory eclogues.   7. Spenser, Edmund, 1552?–1599—Influence. 8. Universities and colleges in literature.   9. Milton, John, 1608–1674. Lycidas.   10. Cambridge (England)—In literature.   11. Clout, Colin (Fictitious character)   12. English poetry—Roman influences.   13. Country life in literature.   I. Title.
    PR509.P3 B68   2000
    821'.309321734—dc21   00-027731

Contents

Preface

Why Tityrus! But you've forgotten me.
I'm Meliboeus the potato man,
The one you had the talk with, you remember,
Here on this very campus years ago.
        —Robert Frost, "Build Soil—A Political Pastoral"

W<small>HETHER ONE REFERS DIRECTLY, OR, AS IN THE ABOVE PASSAGE,</small> obliquely, to the "groves of academe," the inference is invariably an ironic one. Such a description implies more than just a well-cultivated landscape. It infers such enviable pastoral ingredients as boundless leisure, intimate fellowship, and enticing discourse. Hence, the irony. Whether or not, and to what extent, such ingredients have ever actually been a part of academic life, from its earliest origins forward, is only a marginal consideration of the following chapters. More to the point of this study is the fact that many former inhabitants of the academic world have, often without irony, recalled their collegiate experience in pastoral descriptions. There is a significant relationship between the university world of late sixteenth- and early seventeenth-century England and the pastoral poetry of its former residents. My intent is not to show that the Renaissance university world was pastoral, but rather, that Renaissance pastoral poetry is, in large measure, academic: that, Samuel Johnson's derision notwithstanding, the "poetry of pastoral process" does, as Susan Snyder says, "express something real" (147). That something, I hope to show in the chapters that follow, is what Snyder refers to in passing as "the cradling familiarities of Cambridge" (148), which afforded a recollected locus of both spatial and temporal pastoral. English pastoralists, I suggest, reimagined their collegiate environment—its rivalry, poverty, fellowship, and true love—as pastoral, and stylized it as such in the worlds of their eclogues.

When Edmund Spenser initiated the pastoral genre in English with his *Shepheardes Calender* in 1579, he did so in conscious imitation of his classical models, Theocritus and Virgil. Those who followed Spenser in this genre adopted him as a model, along with the classical ancestry and European pastoralists such as Jacopo Sannazaro. Since these English pastorals are not simply the old classics in a new tongue, the question ought to be asked: what, precisely, besides the language, makes English pastoral "English?" Or, to put it another way, what did Spenser and others incorporate into their notion of the idyllic that was not part of their classical models, and what was the source for these particular idyllic ingredients?

Spenser's shepherds are not sheepherders. They discourse eloquently, sing splendidly, enjoy unbounded land and leisure, and are in danger of stepping only in another shepherd's sorrows. The interpretive questions have rightly been: who are these shepherds and where are their fields? A partial and partially correct answer has traditionally been: English courtiers and English court politics. My own assertion challenges this pastoral-court connection that has been at the center of nearly all historical considerations of pastoral for well over a decade. In reasserting the shepherd-courtier allegory with new historical vigor, critics have done much to help us understand the poet's fashioning of himself and his work toward a political future. However, the presumed power preoccupation by which these poets have been judged has, I believe, caused readers to neglect the place from which such poetry springs—namely, the poet's past, which in the case of Spenser and his pastoral followers returns us to the Cambridge they had left behind, not the court at which they never really arrived.

A resident of Pembroke College from 1569 to 1576, Spenser composed his *Shepheardes Calender* in the years immediately following his departure from Cambridge. Spenser's chief imitator in the pastoral genre, Phineas Fletcher, remained at King's College off and on from 1600 to 1615, and chronicled those years in his *Piscatorie Eclogues*, where "Chamus boys" battle for boats and linger in conversation along the banks of the River Cam. John Milton's "Lycidas," his most famous early work, was published four years after Fletcher's *Eclogues* in response to the drowning of a companion Milton had known at Christ's College, where he was a student from 1625 to 1632.

In characterizing the essentially nostalgic, personal, and ekphrastic nature of these three poems, I have found myself reasserting as well the other generic elements that characterize "classical" pastoral. For although pastoral poetry has been described as everything from a mode to a mood, from a strict literary form to a human impulse, with all variations in between, there remain relatively few poems fashioned in deliberate imitation of the eclogues of Theocritus and Virgil. The connection from which this study springs is that these three poems, which are arguably the most successful English imitations of these familiar classical predecessors, are linked as well by their authors' common residence at Cambridge University. Counting this as more than a coincidence, this study draws attention to the relationship of these poets' pastoral worlds and the recollected university world that they inhabited.

Using historical framework, university records, official statutes, and anecdotal details, I attempt to reconstruct a version of the university world that these three poets departed and subsequently reimagined within stylized pastoral constructs. This exploration of the potential origins for "the delights of youth generally" serves as a preface to the subsequent chapters' specific treatment of the poets' pastoral works where the campus becomes a *campus*, a field of pastoral play where students are swains, pens are pipes, and a prolonged conversation in a cloister or corridor is an intimate discourse beneath the shade of the *locus amoenus*, the idyllic place of the spirit. My assertion that English pastoral poetry is the product of sixteenth- and seventeenth-century university life offers an alternative to many of the present explanations of this poetry, which tend to see it as high politics dressed in lowly weeds. My hope is that in reading the following chapters the reader will come nearer to the pastoral impulse, which is in its origins and effect ultimately more personal than political.

Colin's Campus

1

The Pastoralist's Past

The Backward Look

Increasingly, critics have relied upon what we know of the particular goings-on at the court of Queen Elizabeth to explain all things that we call Elizabethan, including a rather gigantic corpus of poetry. Pastoral poetry in particular, long regarded as an allegorical embodiment of court politics, is seen more than ever as the poetic product of social and political power struggles.[1] The central claim of this present study is that the pastoral poetry of Renaissance England has more to do with the academic world than with the world of the court, for although this poetry furnished entertainment for the court, it was born of the academy where Edmund Spenser and others encountered the pastorals of Theocritus and Virgil. In initiating pastoral as an English genre, Spenser looked to these poets to see *how* to write, but, like them, he relied upon his own experience to inform him of *what* to write. The recollection and depiction of pastoral delights not only returned the poet to his well-practiced readings of Virgil and Theocritus, but returned him as well to the place where he first contemplated imitation of those ancient pastoral predecessors, and the moment when he first imagined himself and his native English language as capable of following in their tradition. In his classical models Spenser found the shepherd's *campus*; in his own recollections he found a student's campus. In his English pastoral, and in the pastorals of those who followed him in this genre, the two campuses combine to form a poetry whose new ingredients distinguish it from its classical origins.

What the renewed interest in pastoral as a courtly construct has ignored is that from Theocritus's first eclogue on, pastoral is born of the backward glance.[2] This essentially reflective quality of pastoral poetry is significant to the present study. My assertion that the

13

pastoral worlds of Edmund Spenser, Phineas Fletcher, and John
Milton come from these poets' recollections of their time at Cambridge University rests in part upon the larger claim that all pastoralists find their subject matter by looking backward. Nostalgia is
not only the essential impulse of what I have dubbed the "academic" pastoral, but of all pastoral poetry.

This is not to suggest that either pastoral or one's university years
are without future considerations. On the contrary, one's university
years, spent for the most part in uncovering and developing youthful potential, look as much to the future as to the present. This is
precisely why the pastoralist's recollection of those years looks
with such interest to the past. Recalling a former potential, which
has now presumably taken shape in some "profession," the poet
finds assurance in the backward look that preceded his present maturity. The forward look, by contrast, toward, say, epic poet or fa-
vored courtier, displaces the assurance of recollection with
unutterable anxiety. Colin Clout ceases to sing at the thought of it.
The Shepheardes Calender, as I will argue further in chapter 3, records the complex poetic paralysis of such backward and forward
posturing.

Clearly, the *Calender*, like its author, was fashioned for a world
beyond the confines of the collegiate cloister. Even so, the world
of the *Calender*, wherein reside "the delights of youth generally,"[3]
shares more in common with the enclosed gardens of the poet's
personal past—Pembroke College—than with the political world
where he had begun to forge his poetic future. We come nearer the
English pastoralists' imagination, I believe, by doing as they themselves did, and turning our attention from the complexities of the
greater world back to the safer locus of the university, where the
poet first discovered his own poetic talent, as well as a poetic tradition that affirmed that talent and gave it form.

Looking backward to his or her tradition is a first step for any
poet. Such a search gives the poet the proper form for his subject
matter. Where pastoral poetry is concerned, Virgil looks back to
Theocritus and Spenser looks back to them both;[4] soon English
poets are looking backward to Spenser and pastoral has become a
British genre. This look backward to find the proper form for ideas
is the basis of all genre formation. The poet requires, however,
some lived experience to pour into the shell of the selected convention—some substance from which to fashion a self. In no case is
this more true than in pastoral poetry. As Renato Poggioli points

out, Virgil, Spenser, and the others "followed Theocritus' example in the pastoral, not only in conformity with the tradition of literary imitation, but also as a means to moral relaxation and moral release" (4): to satisfy, in other words, some Epicurean impulses of their very own. For, "even more keenly than Theocritus perhaps, the English poets of the Renaissance found a pure though nostalgic pleasure in contemplating the life of the countryside" (Kermode, 43). This nostalgic contemplation, this introspective look backward to an actual place and time, yields a pastoral world that exists, paradoxically but necessarily, outside of place and time.

"To establish that nostalgia is the basic emotion of pastoral," Laurence Lerner begins "almost at the beginning" with Virgil's first eclogue (41). In this eclogue Tityrus has been granted the *libertas* of keeping his land. His fellow shepherd Meliboeus, on the other hand, is exiled from familiar streams to the thirsty lands of Africa. At his departure Meliboeus delivers a dreamy description of the idyllic world that Tityrus will enjoy. Thus the first description of the pastoral world in Virgil is given by one who is leaving it. Looking backward Meliboeus pastoralizes the land where he has lived:

> Lucky old man! here by familiar streams
> And hallowed springs you'll seek out cooling shade.
> Here for you always, bees from the neighboring hedge,
> Feeding on willow blossoms, will allure
> To slumber soft with sweet murmurings.
> The hillside pruner will serenade the air;
> Nor will the throaty pigeons, your dear care,
> Nor turtledoves cease moaning in the elms.
>
> (I.51–58)[5]

Whether or not Meliboeus ever inhabited such an ideal world, he most certainly leaves one behind. Likewise, whether or not Tityrus's future days will be spent enjoying the cooling shade and nature's perpetual serenades is irrelevant. The pastoral world of Eclogue I is the product of Meliboeus's nostalgic imagination, and as such it belongs more to him than to Tityrus. The loss that initiates Virgil's *Eclogues* is the loss of pastoral itself.

Virgil himself looks backward to his pastoral predecessor Theocritus, whose idylls are filled with reminiscence that, as Edmund Chambers suggests, was born of the poet's own lost landscape.

"Upon Theocritus, a lover of the country, trapped in the bustling decadent city and court life of Ptolemaic Egypt, those bucolic rhythms, remembered so well from his childhood, had all the fascination which the simple exercises over the complex, a fascination wrought out of contrast and reminiscence" (xxii). A native of Sicily, Theocritus exhibited his homesickness in such oddities as the personification of Sicily as the Cyclops.[6] As for the "bustling" of Alexandria, Theocritus's bucolic poems owe more to its libraries than its courts. Hence, his pastoral verse is more self-consciously personal than that of Virgil, which is inseparable from Augustan politics.

In Theocritus's first idyll he creates three separate artifices that are the product of loss. First, there is the idyll itself, in which Thyrsis is stirred to song by a nostalgic appeal from a goatherd: "you, Thyrsis, used to sing 'The Affliction of Daphnis' as well as any man."[7] This recollection is matched by two other pieces of art within the poem that recall the past, in the depiction which Theocritus demonstrates a masterful use of ekphrasis. As a reward for his singing, Thyrsis is offered "a fine great mazer" by the goatherd. The cup contains detailed carving of an idyllic world. A predecessor of Keats's "cold pastoral," this wooden pastoral consists of "curling ivy" and "a woman fashioned as a God might fashion her." We see an old fisher whose "strength is the strength of youth," and "there's a vineyard well laden with clusters red to the ripening, and a little lad seated watching upon the hedge" (I.45–47). The loveliness of this world is matched by its utter unattainability. Twice removed from us, its existence lies within carved wood inside fashioned words. Then there is the song Tityrus sings, "The Affliction of Daphnis," which recounts the death of Daphnis at the hands of Cypris, and laments his loss. Lost too is all harmony in nature: "Pines may grow figs now Daphnis dies, and hind tear hound if she will" (I.135).

This nostalgic sense of loss on the part of the poet, delivered here by Theocritus at three ekphrastic removes, is not incidental to pastoral poetry—it is the reason for the creation of pastoral poetry. As Marinelli describes it: "The great characteristic of pastoral poetry is that it is written when an ideal or at least more innocent world is felt to be lost, but not so wholly as to destroy the memory of it or to make some imaginative intercourse between present reality and past perfection impossible" (9). A pastoralized version of one's own youth is the lost ideal that I believe propels the three poems I will be treating in the coming chapters.

In making this claim, I do not disregard the longing for a Golden Age or a prelapsarian Eden, but reassert the lesson in retrospective discovery taught by Raymond Williams. In the opening chapter of *The Country and the City*, Williams takes the reader on an "escalator ride" back through history. Taking poets at their word when they lament for a former age when life was sweeter, Williams returns to that former age only to discover other poets making similar laments. These poets direct us to still an earlier age, and so on without success. We never arrive at the purported splendor of the days gone by. Long before Williams, Gabriel Harvey employed the identical rationale to admonish Spenser for his naive longing for earlier, more golden, times: "Sir, yower newe complaynte of ye newe worlde is nye as owlde as Adam and Eve, and full as staleist fashion that hath bene in fassion sine Noes fludd . . . there be infinite thousands of examples to proove that the first men in ye worlde were as well ower masters in villanye as ether predecessors in tyme of fathers in consanguitye" (*Letter Book*, 82–83).

Following his own particular search for the blissful Old Englands described by the poets of each succeeding generation, Raymond Williams resolves: "The apparent resting places, the successive Old Englands to which we are confidently referred but which then start to recede, have some actual significance, when they are looked at in their own terms" (12). Williams finds those terms, not surprisingly, in the poets' own youth: "we notice their location in the childhoods of their authors, and this must be relevant. Nostalgia, it can be said, is universal and persistent; only other men's nostalgia offends" (12).[8]

The nostalgia of a good poet, however, need not necessarily offend. It may, in fact, delight. For example, consider a poet's nostalgic remembrance of his first acquaintance with the work of another poet, or his recollection of an initial, inspired appreciation of a particular work ("On First Reading Chapman's Homer"). Such nostalgia has more than once been the source of excellent poetry.

That nostalgia which offends (be it another person's or no) is that which remains essentially nostalgic—that is, nostalgia that does not move beyond its own reminiscence because it does not perceive, let alone attempt to solve, the central problem the pastoral poet faces: how to, in some fashion, preserve what has been lost? The wrong answer to this question—take Jay Gatsby's word for it—is more

detrimental than no answer at all. All pastoral is essentially involved in confronting this problem, and what separates pastoral
poetry from poetry that merely contains pastoral ingredients (a fair
portion of anyone's literary canon) is the solution it offers to the
human problem of loss. The pastoralist's response may be seen in
the offer the goatherd makes to Thyrsis for his labor in song: You
sing about the loss of Daphnis, that we may once again recover him,
and I'll give you this lovely cup. By your song, we shall once again
have Daphnis, though we have him not. And in this cup, you may
have this perfect, unchanging world (sans death), though you have
it not. The pastoral solution, in other words, is invariably an ekphrastic one. Ekphrasis is the device that allows the reader/viewer
to have and have not. It recovers the past, makes it perfect, and at
the same time announces itself explicitly as artifice.

Longus, the third-century author of the pastoral romance *Daphnis and Chloe*, offers the clearest use of pastoral ekphrasis I know
in his painted picture of a tale of love. His story, he tells us, is one
that he received from an interpreter of a delightful painting inside
of a beautiful grove that he happened across once upon a time:

> Once while I was hunting in Lesbos I saw in a grove of the Nymphs the
> fairest sight I have ever seen. It was the painted picture of a tale of love.
> The grove itself was beautiful; it was thick with trees, and abounding in
> flowers, all well-watered by a single fountain which brought refresh-
> ment to both alike. But more delightful still was that picture, both for
> its consummate art and for its tale of love. Its fame drew many visitors,
> even from a distance, to supplicate the Nymphs and to view the paint-
> ing. In it were represented women in childbed, and others fitting swad-
> dling clothes upon infants. There were sheep nursing them and
> shepherds taking them up; there were young lovers pledging faith to one
> another, an incursion of pirates, an attack by invaders. All these scenes
> spoke of love, and as I looked upon and admired them I conceived a
> strong desire to compose a literary pendant to that painted picture. Upon
> inquiry I found an interpreter of the picture, and I have carefully set the
> story out in four books, as an offering to Eros, the Nymphs, and Pan,
> and as a delightful possession for all mankind.[9]

The world of Longus's tale, like the world upon Thyrsis's cup, belongs entirely to us if we could only have it. It resides in a story
transcribed from an oral narrative of a picture in a grove whose locale is as remote and idyllic as the world of the tale itself. Thus,
even while he sets his work in time and place, the author of this

prose romance imitates the pastoralist, who negates both time and place, leaving us with a world that we describe, however inadequately, as pastoral. The deliberate refashioning of one's personal loss into a remote (though curiously tangible) world is the art of the pastoralist inherited by English poets.

One final aspect of this refashioned world bears mentioning before turning to the particular circumstances of the English pastoralists in this study. The backward glance notwithstanding, utopian and pastoral ingredients do inevitably intertwine. Although the "places" of pastoral are not those of future possibility, but of remembered past, this is not to say that certain readers might not look to pastoral settings with a mind bent toward an idyllic future. Likewise, some imagined utopian worlds do indeed contain pastoral ingredients—"The lion shall lie down with the lamb." Boring an audience with one's personal nostalgia, therefore, is the least of the potential offenses of the pastoral enterprise. Worse by far is the crime of inciting riot. As Alan Hager has observed, pastoral as a "transcendent ideal envisages a collective society . . . where joint activity and sharing make human life for once supportable, without hierarchy and its concomitant police force" (118). In his discussion of what he calls "the mirage of the Green World," Hager examines how Shakespeare, in *As You Like It* and *The Winter's Tale,* critiques the very idyllic green worlds he creates. In contrast to Karl Marx's nineteenth-century utopian call for proletarian unity, Hager argues, Shakespeare's presentations of ideal collectivism carry an embedded ironic distancing that, like Longus's and Theocritus's artistic framing, makes clear to the reader and the would-be revolutionary: *you can't get there from here.* Even so, neither Shakespeare nor any other artist can stop people from wanting to go there, and, as every English teacher knows, irony is never universally discernible. Ever since Eve's unfortunate consumption of the fruit of knowledge, we share, for better or worse, some version of the notion that "we've got to get ourselves back to the garden," and any presentation of the idyllic, a cautious Samuel Johnson would remind us, shares the responsibility for luring people there.

However, the distinction between pastoral and utopian literature is a real one, and one that is too frequently overlooked. William Empson runs into this trouble as he works to untangle proletarian literature from pastoral literature. "My own difficulty about proletarian literature," he says, "is that when it comes off I find I am taking it as pastoral literature; I read into it, or find that the author has secretly put into it, these more subtle, more far-reaching, and I think more permanent, ideas" (20). By more permanent ideas Empson presumably means ideas that, by their very stability, are more a part of the past than of a world yet to come. Pastoral may well be incorporated into proletarian literature. Pastoral is incorporated into all kinds of things.[10] It turns up (and even more often remains unnoticed) where people least expect it. But if proletarian were being incorporated into pastoral, what we would have in that case would no longer be pastoral. For pastoral does not aim to suggest future possibilities of justice, peace, or harmony. Pastoral is certainly about such things, but it finds them by looking backward. Lions lying down with lambs may be a pastoral ingredient, but it is a utopian concept.

While Spenser and his fellow pastoralists were not dabbling in an enterprise nearly as volatile as Shakespeare in the public playhouses of London, they nonetheless shared both the paradoxes and complex ironic distancing of his age. Imbedded critique as explicit as Jacques's or irony as acerbic as Touchstone's was not a necessary precaution in a well-framed artifice like the pastoral eclogue, but, as we shall see, self-critique is an inherent pastoral ingredient in the pastoral argument. One additional distancing of the pastoral eclogue from the political desire of collective idealism is the fact that the more genuinely pastoral a poem is, the more inevitably personal it is as well.

Each of the three poets whom I consider in the coming chapters confronted, like Theocritus and Virgil before them, the personal predicament of loss as they departed the cloistered world of youth, the university, for the greater world of responsibility. In Theocritus's *Idylls*, a relatively recent addition to their curriculum, these English pastoralists saw the "invention" of bucolic poetry and the strong sense of personal loss that accompanied that invention. In the more familiar *Eclogues* of Virgil, these same poets recognized a circumstance more like their own, in which the very creation of idyllic poetry was dependent upon the grace of a decidedly civil power structure.

Using the form of a calendar, itself a frozen, and inadequate, measure of that which inevitably passes, Edmund Spenser initiated pastoral as an English genre, all the while confronting himself the essential pastoral question of personal loss. He had recently departed from Pembroke College, where his closest companion, Gabriel Harvey, remained behind. Now living in Kent, Spenser fashioned himself as Colin Clout, Harvey as Hobbinol, and turned his former residence into a pastoralized paradise from which he was unhappily removed. As Meliboeus addressed Tityrus, so Colin addresses Hobbinol:

> That paradise hast found, whych Adam lost.
> Here wander may thy flock early or late,
> Withouten dreade of Wolues to bene ytost:
> Thy louely layes here mayst thou freely boste.
> But I unhappy man, whom cruell fate,
> And angry Gods pursue from coste to coste,
> Can nowhere fynd, to shroude my lucklesse pate.
>
> (June, 10–16)

As Colin, Spenser recollects the less complicated, careless days of his youth—"I whylst youth, and course of carelesse yeeres" (June, 33). Forgetting the accompanying miseries of his college days—as we are all wont to do—he re-creates not only a perfect place and time for song, but the perfect companion with whom to sing. This recollection, as Harvey will point out, has no more to do with the world in which Harvey actually lives than does Meliboeus's sorrow-inspired depiction of his former residence where fortunate Tityrus now resides.

Mired in the particularly anti-pastoral enterprise of battling for academic rank at Trinity College, Harvey challenges his friend's intoxicated recollection. Taking the occasion of a pastoral revelry of his own—"at myne hostisses by the fyresyde being faste heggid in rownde abowte on every side with a company of honest good fellowes, and reasonable honeste quaffers"—Gabriel Harvey sets to dispelling from his friend's idealistic mind thoughts of past and present golden worlds:

> You suppose the first age was the goulde age. It is nothinge soe . . . You suppose us students happye, and thinke the aire praeferrid that breath-ithe on thes same greate lernid philosophers and profonde clarkes. Would to god you were on of these men but a sennighte. I dowbte not but you would sweare ere Sundaye nexte, that there were not the like wofull and miserable creatures to be fownde within ye cumpas of the whole worlde agayne. (86–87)

This is a long way from the opening lines of the June Eclogue, in which Hobbinol declares: "Lo Colin, here the place, whose pleas-

ant syte / From other shades hath weand my wandring mynde." The
Hobbinol who proclaims this is, like the locus he describes, the
product of the pastoralist's imagination—a Colin Clout who perceives as idyllic the world that he (quite literally) can no longer inhabit. This paradise is not Kent, nor merely "the southpartes," but
the poet's reimagined Pembroke, an irretrievable time as place, a
locus amoenus for which Colin, by his very aspirations, is no longer
suited, and where his closest companion remains behind. Louise
Schleiner, in her argument for E. K. as a Harvey-Spenser construct,
describes the circumstance perfectly: "The effect for Harvey as he
read the printed *Calender* must have been stirring: a recognition
that his student and devoted friend had now outgrown him. By con-
tinuing their friendship in this new situation, he justifies his place
in the *locus amoenus* of 'June' as definer of the young scholar-
poet's earlier paradise of expression and learning" (396).[11]

While a collegiate reading of *The Shepheardes Calender* must
rely in some measure upon the elaborate construct of E. K.'s gloss,
the *Piscatorie Eclogues* of Spenser's imitator, Phineas Fletcher, are
explicitly academic. Nowhere more than on Fletcher's "River
Cam" are the academic and pastoral campuses more overtly connected. Like his father before him, Fletcher was denied the privilege of being a fellow at Cambridge, and his eclogues record both
his and his father's academic misfortunes. Like Virgil and Spenser
before him, Fletcher's idyllic world springs from the recollections
of a departing swain, Thirsil (Phineas Fletcher), addressing his
dearest companion, Thomalin (John Tompkins), who remains behind in that world:

> Farewell ye streams, which once I loved deare;
> Farewell ye boyes, which on your Chame do float;
> Muses farewell, if there be Muses here;
> Farewell my nets; farewell my little boat:
>   My Thomalin, with thee all sweetnesse dwell;
>   Think of thy Thirsil, Thirsil loves thee well.
> Thomalin, my dearest deare, my Thomalin farewell.
>
>   (II.24)[12]

In what amounts to a piscatory rendition of Colin Clout's "adieu
delights," Thirsil here catalogues simultaneously the academic and
pastoral joys that his companion, but not he, may enjoy.

The most famous companionless shepherd in pastoral poetry,

however, is the uncouth swain of Milton's "Lycidas," who, though he comes forth alone, recollects, like Meliboeus, Colin and Thirsil before him, the world and the friendship that he and his companion had formerly shared:

> For we were nursed upon the self-same hill,
> Fed the same flock, by fountain, shade and rill.
> Together both, ere the high lawns appeared
> Under the opening eyelids of the Morn,
> We drove a-field, and both together heard
> What time the grey-fly winds her sultry horn,
> Oft till the star that rose at evening bright
> Toward heaven's descent had sloped his westering wheel.
>
> (23–31)

The imbedded academic allegory in this passage caused Samuel Johnson to complain: "We know that they [Edward King and Milton] never drove afield, and that they had no flock to batten" (*Lives*, I.164). John Milton, in other words, was no shepherd. He was, however, a student together with Edward King: "The hill . . . is, of course, Cambridge; the joint feeding of flocks is companionship in study; the rural ditties on the oaten flute are academic iambics and elegiacs."[13] Like Phineas Fletcher and John Tompkins before them, and Edmund Spenser and Gabriel Harvey before that, Milton and King shared an irretrievable time and place that, though far less than idyllic, could be recollected and re-created so in pastoral poetry.

In asserting a connection between these poets' pastorals and their collegiate experience, one must look carefully to both campuses, that is, insofar as possible, the actual world of the poet's youthful experience, and, even more importantly, the poet's recollected version of that world. The university world in sixteenth- and seventeenth-century England, for example, was experiencing a fluctuation between medieval Catholicism and Protestant secularism that might be said to have contained the worst of both worlds. Still predominantly cloistered, clerical, celibate, and monastic in its rules, the emerging university of the Reformation was connected in a new way to the national power structure. Describing this intimacy between the academic and the social world in the Tudor era, Hugh Kearney says:

> Within the college, the student, lay or clerical, was provided with a controlled intellectual and religious environment . . . Tutorial supervision,

which in the twentieth century aims at creating a critical attitude of mind, was in the sixteenth century a form of intellectual and moral discipline. The college reproduced in little the social and intellectual assumptions of the Tudor state. Social divisions among the student body between fellow commoners and sizars reflected those of society at large. The object of education within the colleges was to produce intellectuals and gentlemen who could be relied upon in a world constantly threatened, it was thought, by revolution. (22)

To claim, then, that the academic world of Spenser, Fletcher, and Milton was somehow disconnected from concerns of power and social advancement would be naive. The university owed its very existence to the ruling national power structure in a way that it never had before.

On the other hand, we may rightly ask whether an individual's personal recollection of his or her time spent in such a world is chiefly filled with remembered power negotiations. Such a belief would be as unnecessarily cynical as the former is naive. The speaker in "Lycidas" recalls being nursed upon the selfsame hill, not struggling with others to get to the top of the hill. Likewise, Fletcher, while he documents his own unsuccessful power struggles within the world of Cambridge, depicts those struggles in a world as idyllic as Longus's grove. In the correspondence of Spenser and Harvey, we see that one's naivete or cynicism is furnished in large measure by one's distance from the world one is describing. Spenser, removed from the university world, finds himself in a world of patronage, posts, and unmitigated power games, and reimagines a time and place without such concerns. Harvey remains immersed in the world that Spenser has departed and sees that academic politics are inseparable from the greater world, masters of colleges themselves being court appointments.

The university world that Spenser apparently recollected so fondly in his letter to Harvey is the very one that Dr. Caius, having returned to Cambridge after a twenty-nine year absence, found lamentable. Believing post-Reformation Cambridge to be decayed in manner, order, and dress, Dr. Caius, in 1573 (the year Spenser graduated with a B.A. from Pembroke) offers "pastoral" recollections of his younger days at Cambridge. In winter, he recalls, the newly made bachelors used to wear laurel wreaths. Dr. Caius fancifully derives the very title of "baccalaureus" from the garland that used to be worn. In summer, he remembers, the wreaths were made of flowers and roses: "In my youth no one whatever his rank, presumed, even in salutation, to bare his head or remove his cap, which was esteemed the mark of approved merit. Now alas! roses and flowers are scorned and we parade our wealth by a display of chains and ornaments of gold" (Gray, 100). Colin Clout and Hobbinol sport no such gaudy ornaments or chains. And one could undoubtedly hop upon Williams's escalator to Dr. Caius's own Cambridge of 1529 and find there a lament for the idyllic, rose-filled days of yore. Recollecting garlands where they were not may be a crime that belongs to everyone, but it is an art belonging exclusively to the pastoralists.

THEN AND THERE

Before turning, in the next chapter, to the real world of sixteenth-century Cambridge, I wish to examine in somewhat more detail the art of ekphrastic recollection by which Cambridge was re-created as a world removed from both time and place. The harmonious descriptions given of and by young swains do not include a measure of hours or counting of days, but merely the arrival of a new season. For, seen by the young swains, their world is not so much a place or even a period of time, but an opportunity for song:

> It was the time faithfull Halcyone,
> Once more enjoying new-liv'd Ceyx bed,
> Had left her young birds to the wavering sea,
> Bidding him calm his proud white-curled head,
> And change his mountains to a champian lea;
> The time when gentle Flora's lover reignes,
> Soft creeping all along green Neptunes smoothest plains;
> When haplesse Thelgon (a poore fisher-swain)
> Came from his boat to tell the rocks his plaining.
>
> (I.1–9)

This nostalgic opening to Fletcher's *Eclogues* is a typical pastoral description in which time is no more than the harmonious, and in this case amorous, movement of the gods (a harmony that, as we will see in the case of Phoebus, marks each day's end). What we learn from the nautical mythical allusions above is that the seas were calm, and that it was springtime. The pastoral "place" enjoys a similar anonymity, a nearby spot in the shade or, as in the piscatorial case above, beneath the shelter of an overhanging crag.

Such anti-time and anti-place descriptions do not yield the nowhere of utopias but the embellished somewhere of an irretrievable past; or, if retrievable, remembered only in poetry. The recollection of a nostalgic imagination, for example, can, as Fletcher does here, depict life at Cambridge as an idyllic world outside of time and place; not a world without conflicts, love pangs, or even drownings, but a world in which nature was attuned to, in harmony with, those conflicts and grievings; a world such as Colin Clout describes in the December Eclogue; a world where plenty of fraternal spirit and fellowship had provided a *locus amoenus*, and sufficient occasion for song.

Actual time, the time that requires counting, is capable of destroying such a world. Measured time makes the court go round, but not necessarily the world, and certainly not the pastoral world of these poets. What follows here is an examination of the chronology and geographics, the descriptions of time and place, in the groves of Spenser's *Calender*, on the banks of Fletcher's River Chame, and in the world of the poor swain in Milton's "Lycidas."

As seen above, the season of the year is often as close to time as we get in the pastoral world. The poet is not so much telling us the time as providing us with a setting. In describing the season, the poet is, as in the case of Spenser's *Calender*, providing a chronology for the poems. However, the poet's aim is not chiefly a narrative one. He is not as concerned with telling us when events are occurring as he is with telling us what the world is like, what sort of songs should be sung. Thus it is that Willye beckons Thomalin in the March Eclogue of *The Shepheardes Calender*:

> Thomalin, why sytten we soe,
> As weren ouerwent with woe,
> Vpon so fayre a morrow?
> The ioyous time now nigheth fast,
> That shall alegge this bitter blast,
> And slake the winters sorowe.

> (March, 1–6)

Willye is not warning his friend of the passing of time or alerting him to a time-imposed action. Rather, he is calling his friend out of one mood and into another. Thomalin's reply indicates his new awareness, not of the time so much as the place, the setting about him that has begun to change:

> Sicker Willye, thou warnest well:
> For Winters wrath beginnes to quell,
> And pleasant spring appeareth.
> The grasse now ginnes to be refresht,
> The swallow peepes out of her nest,
>   And clowdie Welkin cleareth.
>
> (7–12)

The setting that the season has begun to yield calls for a love song, in this case a love lament on the part of Thomalin, whose mood cannot match the season's. As we will see later, because he is in disharmony with the season, he also marks time within the course of his lament. For now, though, let us look at another "time," the season opposite of March in the *Calender*, November. Here, as in March, the shepherd's concern is not with the progression or arrival of time, but with what song should be sung in what setting.

Asked by Thenot for a song, Colin Clout replies:

> Thenot, now nis the time of merimake.
> Nor Pan to herye, nor with loue to playe:
> Sike myrth in May is meetest for to make,
> Or summer shade vnder the cocked haye.
> But nowe sadde Winter welked hath the day,
> And Phoebus weary of his yerely taske,
> Ystabled hath his steedes in lowlye laye,
> And taken vp his ynne in Fishes haske.
> Thilke sollein season sadder plight doth aske.
>
> (November, 9–17)

Just as Thomalin provides a description of early spring by describing the changes in the world around him, so Colin does with the last stages of autumn. Neither shepherd is as concerned with the time as with what their newly changed world awakens in them. As Thomalin responds with a love complaint, Colin responds appropriately with an elegy for Dido in which he confirms: "Now is time to dye" (81).

In a more substantial elegy, the swain of "Lycidas" begins with an apology for singing his dirge out of season. It is apparently summer and he tells the deities:

I come to pluck your [Laurels and Myrtils] Berries harsh and crude,
And with forc'd fingers rude,
Shatter your leaves before the mellowing year.
Bitter constraint, and sad occasion dear
Compels me to disturb your season due.

(3–5)

Time, in this case, is something with which the shepherd is out of
synchrony, something he disturbs with his own disharmony.

Each of the above worlds possesses an element of timelessness in
that the shepherd or fisher swains are concerned not with the passing of time, but with the changes time has wrought in their world.
Time is not something of which to keep track, but something with
which to be apart. The shepherd's concern is not to be somewhere
on time, but to be in time with somewhere—that is, to be in harmony with the season. As a creator of settings and shaper of moods,
pastoral time functions ekphrastically, forming part of a stasis that
is free of the change narrative progression might create. This stasis
is additionally formed by the anonymity of place (the locale of *The
Shepheardes Calender* is as vaguely idyllic as Longus's painted tale
of love), and even of person:

A shepeheards boye (no better doe him call)
When Winters wastful spight was almost spent,
All in a sunneshine day, as did befall,
Led forth his flock, that had bene long ypent.

(January, l.1–4)

The shepherd speaks his complaint, smashes his pipe, and beckons
to his sheep—all of which can be frozen not just in the woodcut,
but in the eclogue form.

A similar anonymity is found in the June Eclogue of the *Calender* in Colin's address to happier shepherds: "Ye gentle shepheards,
which your flocks do feede, / Whether on hylls, or dales, or other
where" (l.106–7). This "other where" may be beneath a tree "in
secreate shade alone" (December, l.5–6). Or, in the case of the
fisher swains, beneath another shade: "About his head a rocky
canopie, / And craggy hangings round a shadow threw, / Rebutting
Phoebus parching fervencie" (*Piscatorie Eclogues*, I.3.1.1–3). Just
as these worlds are free of the particular encroachments of time, so
too as places they remain nameless. They are found roughly within
the vicinity of the poet's embellished memory.

The world of "Lycidas" is just such a memory not bothered by the bounds of actual time and place. The anonymous uncouth swain sings his lament for the drowned Lycidas, recalling in nostalgic fashion their former days together. Presumably the two young Cambridge students, Milton and Edward King, had places to be on occasion and clocks and bells to call them there. Recollected and re-created as a pastoral existence, however, actual time and place disappear and are replaced with idyllic descriptions (quoted above) that caused Dr. Johnson to laugh at the portrayal of Milton and King as undergraduates, pasturing the "same flock" on "the self-same hill."

It has been suggested that "Lycidas" expresses a nostalgic longing on the part of John Milton for the old gods of mythology. Whether or not this is so, as an ekphrastic image "Lycidas" depicts the nostalgic longing on the part of an older John Milton for a younger John Milton. In re-creating the world of Cambridge where he and King were classmates, Milton has used familiar timeless and placeless markings that we have seen already in the passages from Spenser and Fletcher. The time is the season before the long grasses grew, and the nameless swains feed their flock by the anonymous "fountain, shade and rill." They come afield before the opening eye-lids of the morning, hear the insect hum of midday, and often stay, not only until the evening dew is formed, but even into the latter part of the night, when the evening begins its western descent.[14] It was not, we presume, a matter of losing track of time; for as in the other worlds of idyllic recollection there is no time other than the harmonious moving forward of nature.

Explaining Epicurus's term *galene* (a term that, appropriately enough in regards to Fletcher's piscatory world, means "calm of the storm"), T. G. Rosenmeyer comments: "The Epicurean invocation of calm is assisted by the axiom that there is, objectively speaking, no time. The present is all; memories and hopes are insubstantial; time relations are merely secondary functions of body and place" (70). This timelessness, as Rosenmeyer notes, dates back to Theocritus: "The Theocritean herdsmen is not aware of time as fleeting; he merely proceeds with a special kind of unself-conscious urgency" (86). Such unself-conscious urgency is found in the narrator and his friends in Theocritus's seventh idyll. On their way to a harvest home, the three are overtaken by Lycidas, a goatherd, who asks: "What Simichidas . . . whither away this sultry noontide, when e'en the lizard will be sleeping i' th' hedge and the

crested larks go not afield?" (1.21–23). As if to show that time is of
no concern to them, they reply by inviting Lycidas to a singing
match that goes on for several pages.

We begin to see here what the pastoralists' recollected world provides its characters. Instead of the standard depictions of time and
place that restrict most literary settings, pastoral characters are
placed more vaguely in a pleasant place and given an unboundaried
occasion for song. We, not they, are particularly conscious of the
frame, the cup, the picture, the verse that contains them. The framing of characters in such a stasis depends upon their own perception. When, for example, Colin Clout speaks of the former world
he has lost, it is not an idyllic place from which he has been removed, but an idyllic time, a time "of carelesse yeeres." What
Colin has lost in his failed love pursuit is an idyllic outlook. He has
discovered unfaithfulness. Unlike the naively carefree Hobbinol,
Colin is now all too conscious of time, which "in passing weares"
just as garments—time, which brings about "ryper age" and
"hoary heares." As we will see in chapter three, Colin, as he increases the distance between himself and the world of the *Calender*,
becomes conscious of the framed artifice in which he moves, or
rather, stands.

The dialogue between Colin and Hobbinol reveals not just the
price of maturity, but the very transient nature of the *locus amoenus*. The *locus amoenus* is not exclusively for the young, but young
people are the only ones perhaps completely unaware of its transient nature. Hobbinol has rediscovered Adam's Eden, and we
know how easily such gardens are lost. What Hobbinol sees now,
with youthful eyes, is only what is all around him. He cannot understand Colin's inability to enter this world, and can only regret
Colin's refusal to sing. Colin cannot sing because he cannot enter
the place for song; he can only recall in a lament his former singing.
Colin, outside of, or beyond, this *locus amoenus*, no longer enjoys
the carefree peace of youth, and speaks instead of time and its
passing.

In the April Eclogue we find the shepherd's perfect excuse for
pastoral pause. Hobbinol, having told of Colin's loss to a scorning
lover, is invited by Thenot to sing one of the songs that Colin will
sing no more:

> But if hys ditties bene so trimly dight,
> I pray thee Hobbinoll, recorde some one:

> The whiles our flockes doe graze about in sight,
> And we close shrowded in thys shade alone.
>
> (1.29–32)

It is not, as in the case of the forsaken lover, that time passes te-
diously while the sheep graze, but rather that their grazing provides
the time and place for these shep herds to "worke delyte." The
fisher swain enjoys a similar excuse in his "work," which Izaak
Walton calls "the contemplative man's vocation": "There while
our thinne nets dangling in the winde / Hung on our oars tops, I
learnt to sing" (*Piscatorie Eclogues*, I.6.1–2). There is no particular
need for holidays in either of these worlds. The "work" of both the
shepherd and the fisher swain provides a built-in pause of leisure
that may be filled with song or conversation. When the "work" is
interrupted by weather, this is but another excuse for singing.

When, in the September Eclogue of the *Calender*, Hobbinol en-
counters the misfortunes of Diggon Dauie, he finds that "nowe the
Westerne wind bloweth sore" (49) and, with true pastoral courtesy,
he invites Diggon to shelter and to conversation:

> Sitte we downe vnder the hill:
> Tho may we talke, and tellen our fill,
> And make a mocke at the blustring blast.
> Now say on Diggon, what euer thou hast.
>
> (52–55)

To the distraught Diggon, the storm echoes his misfortunes. For
Hobbinol, it is the occasion for stormy conversation, which mocks
the "blustring blast" of troubles out in the world from which he has
invited his fellow shepherd to retreat. While not on the surface of it
a *locus amoenus*, the shelter from the storm serves, no less than the
shade by the grazing sheep, as a place apart. The autumn storm is
in its season, what the tree's shade is in spring, a reason for pause
from the world to indulge in song or the fellowship of conversation.

A storm is also the occasion for piscatory pause in the second of
Fletcher's *Eclogues*, when Dorus invites Myrtil to song:

> Myrtil, why idle sit we on the shore?
> Since stormy windes, and waves intestine spite
> Impatient rage of sail, or bending oare;
> Sit we, and sing, while windes & waters fight;
> And carol lowd of love, and loves delight.
>
> (1.1–5)

This stormy setting, certainly not the *locus amoenus* that Hobbinol describes in June of the *Calender*, is cousin to the retreat of Hobbinol and Diggon from the September storm. In both cases, this time spent sheltering from the storm is, so far as the narrative is concerned, a place apart. Just as Diggon uses the occasion to lament the abuses done to him, and to disclose ecclesiastical scandal, so Myrtil suggests similar misfortunes as the subject of song during the rage of storms: "Dorus, ah rather stormy seas require / With sadder song the tempests rage deplore: / In calms let's sing of love, and lovers fire" (2.6–8). He goes on to sing of academic rather than ecclesiastical scandal, describing Thirsil's departure from Chame's ungrateful shores.

In defiance of his own prescription, Myrtil uses the occasion of a storm in the very next Eclogue to sing of "lovers fire," namely, his own. In an opening strongly echoing the opening to the January Eclogue in the *Calender*,[15] Fletcher again uses the storm of the world as the occasion for song. His piscatory portrait depicts the fisherman's idleness amidst the storm that rages about him.

> A Fisher-lad (no higher dares he look)
> Myrtil, sat down by Silver Medwayes shore:
> His dangling nets (hung on the trembling oare)
> Had leave to play, so had his idle hook,
> While madding windes the madder Ocean shook.
>
> (III.1.1–5)

As with the shepherds watching their sheep graze, one has the sense in this description that the nets are not all that have "leave to play."

As we have seen in the circumstance of Colin and Hobbinol, the timelessness of the pastoral world is largely a matter of perception. Hobbinol, as one belonging to the *locus amoenus*, is happily incapable of perceiving the boundary of time that holds youth. He is in company with Cuddie, who tells the aging Thenot in the Februarie Eclogue that although "Age and Winter accord full nie" (27), "my flowring youth is foe to frost, / My shippe vnwont in stormes to be tost" (31–32).

Thenot and Piers, unlike Cuddie and Hobbinol, are swains who are in this world but not entirely of it. They represent in the *Calender* the two forces from the "real world" that most severely threaten the pastoral world—death and love. Thenot has an aging heart, Colin an aching heart. Both of them have traveled beyond the world of youth, and brought back with them, besides their respective ailments, a preoccupation with time.

Thenot's preoccupation is the more understandable as well as the more forgivable: he has grown old; the promise of eternal youth is sham, and the careless ways of Cuddie, utter foolishness. Time is real to Thenot, no longer something to be passed idly, but something to be held onto, to be counted: "Selfe haue I worne out thrise threttie yeares, / Some in much joy, many in many teares" (17–18). A figure like "thrise threttie years," is a measure of time incomprehensible to young swains like Cuddie or Hobbinol, for whom time is something to be passed in merriment, not to be measured.

In the May Eclogue of *The Shepheardes Calender*, Spenser presents us, according to E. K., "the persons of two shepheards Piers and Palinode [in whom] be represented two formes of pastoures or Ministers, or the protestant and the Catholique." Piers, as it turns out, is, strictly speaking, the better pastor, but Palinode, with his envy of the joys of youth, is, it must be confessed, more pastoral. He supplies, in fact, a virtual outline of the pastoral joys for the "mery moneth of May" and asks:

> How shoulden shepheardes liue, if not so?
> What? should they pynen in payne and woe?
> Nay sayd I thereto, by my deare borrowe,
> If I may rest, I nill liue in sorrowe.
> Sorrowe ne neede to be hastened on.
>
> (May, 148–52)

Hobbinol and Cuddie would sooner be followers of Palinode, who, more experienced than they, knows sorrow, and whose prescription for it is essentially *carpe diem*. On the other side stands the unpastoral Piers, who, we should not be surprised to learn, is chiefly concerned with how the young shepherds spend their time:

> Those faytours little regarden their charge.
> While they letting their sheepe runne at large,
> Passen their time, that should be sparely spent,
> In lustihede and wanton meryment.
>
> (May, 39–42)[16]

This preoccupation with time, understandable in a minister, and forgivable in an old man, is less of both in a young swain. Love apparently is one excuse for such a preoccupation, as the fever of love puts the swain into a Petrarchan disharmony with the season:

> No winter now, but in my breast, remaining:
>   Yet feels this breast a summers burning fever:
>   And yet (alas!) my winter thaweth never:
> And yet (alas!) this fire eats and consumes me ever.
>
> (*Piscatorie Eclogues*, V.4.6–9)

The lovestruck seem to find at least some comfort in measuring, as Thomalin does in the March Eclogue of the *Calender*: "For sithens it is but the third morowe, / That I chaunst to fall a sleepe with sorowe / And waked againe with griefe" (46–48).

From the beginning of the *Calender* we find in Colin a lovesick swain enamored as well, apparently, with numbers:

> A thousand sithes I curse that carefull hower
> Wherein I longd the neighbor towne to see:
> And eke tenne thousand sithes I blesse the stoure,
> Wherein I sawe so fayre a sight, as shee.
>
> (January, 49–52)

We find a similar disposition to hyperbolic counting in Myrtil, whom we last left in a storm on Medwayes shore: "Tryphon, that know'st a thousand herbs in vain," he complains, "But know'st not one to cure a love-sick heart" (*Piscatorie Eclogues* III.5.6–7). And what has been banished from his heart but "Late thousand joyes securely lodged there" (III.8.2).

Such counting, though, is not peculiar to lovers. What we find is that any character in disharmony with the pastoral world not only expresses that disharmony but measures it. In the harmony of a seemingly timeless world, such as that of Hobbinol and Cuddie, there could be no more certain indication of disharmony than the marking of time. For when measured time shows up in the pastoral world— that is, when time is described in any terms other than the harmonious movement forward with nature—as in the above passages, the pastoral world as an ekphrasis stasis is threatened, if not destroyed. For ekphrasis is the essential device by which the pastoralist defies time in framing his song. When a swain begins to measure time and speak of other places as Colin does, he is not long for "this" world.

In Fletcher's Eclogue IV, the fisherman Chromis suffers, not from love, but from piscatory (i.e., academic) politics. He makes a lengthy complaint describing the offenses of his fellow fishermen and laments the sad decline of the fisher's trade (i.e., Christian discipleship). As seen from the earlier passages from the piscatory world of Fletcher, the storm is the measure of time, if there be any measure at all. The work of fishing having ceased, the interval is passed in song. In this sad picture of the degenerated world of Chamus, however, time will not be described in terms of the flowing water currents or the coming and departure of one of nature's storms. Rather, with the vanishing of piscatory bliss, the destructive force of actual time asserts itself:

> Thelgon. Chromis my joy, why drop thy rainie eyes?
>   And fullen clouds hang on thy heavie brow?
>   Seems that thy net is rent, and idle lies;
>   Thy merry pipe hangs broken on a bough:
>   But late thy time in hundred joyes thou spent'st;
>   Now time spends thee, while thou in vain lament'st.
> Chromis. Thelgon, my pipe is whole, and nets are new
>   But nets and pipe contemn'd and idle lie:
>   My little reed, that late so merry blew,
>   Tunes sad notes to his masters miserie:
>   Time is my foe, and hates my rugged rimes
>   And I as much hate both that hate, and times.
>   (Eclog 4.1–12)

Two things characterize Chromis's state: lack of harmony—an idle pipe that tunes only sad notes of misery—and the presence of time. Chromis's complaint echoes both the lovesick swain and the aging shepherd. Like the lover, time now passes slowly and is measurable. It spends him, rather than the other way around, and he thus has cause, not just to notice and measure time, but to hate it. Chromis also sounds like the aging shepherd. Like Thenot, he is sadly aware of time's passing and leaving him little to show for it. In this latter sense, time acts as betrayer. It is not his peers who are blamed for hating his rhymes, but Time.

In a passage that echoes this one, we hear similar complaining about the shepherd's trade:

> Alas! What boots it with uncessant care
> To tend the homely slighted Shepherd's trade,
> And strictly meditate the thankless Muse?

> Were it not better done as others use,
> To sport with Amaryllis in the shade,
> Or with the tangles of Neaera's hair?
>
> ("Lycidas," 64–69)

Like Chromis, the uncouth swain of Milton's "Lycidas" here depicts time as a betrayer. No doubt time has hated some of his rhymes, and yielded no fame. Like Chromis, he is both lover and elder, bothered and betrayed by time. He has been urged by the likes of Piers "To scorn delights, and live laborious days" (1.72), but there seems little point in this if the blind furies randomly cut off the likes of Lycidas. "Uncessant care" suggests a shepherd whose world is anything but timeless. Yet, the last three lines indicate a shepherd who has at least heard of Hobbinol and Cuddie, if not enjoyed their company.

The ekphrasis created by the pastoralist depends upon anonymity of time and place for its survival. When the threatening world beyond the pastoral intrudes in the form of unfaithful love, unjust politics, ecclesiastical malfeasance, age, and death, the swain becomes cognizant of his actual place in the world and begins to mark time. The framed locus, no longer still, now vanishes. Until then, time is not measured, but passed in "works of delyte" until "stouping Phoebus steepes his face," at which time, even the contented Willye will conclude: "Yts time to hast vs homeward" (*Calender*, March, 117–18). Phoebus is to the pastoral dialogue what the *deus ex machina* is to the Greek drama. The descent of the sun is less a measuring of time, than a way of harmoniously drawing to a close the argument of an eclogue.[17] The *deus ex machina* at least provides some resolution to the drama, albeit an improbable one. The descent of Phoebus is merely the cyclic action of nature that calls the shepherds from field to home, drawing to an unresolved close both turmoil and joy alike.

The recollection of a real place and time and its subsequent recreation into a framed world protected from such concerns is the essential pastoral response to loss. Edmund Spenser, Phineas Fletcher, and John Milton each offer that response to the loss of the world of their earliest poetic maturity, where they, like the swains they would later create, stood in an initiative world apart from the greater world, a world of potentiality where one might test his songs on peers and elders alike, a world whose cloistering walls and enclosed orchard gardens might later make for green cabinets indeed. My aim in the following chapters is to steer between extremes of naivete and cynicism by first offering an understanding, as well as one can, of the university world that these poets inhabited, and then to see that world again as it was recollected and framed in verse.

2

The Campus

IN THE MID-TWELFTH CENTURY THE POPULAR AGRICULTURAL FESTI-
vals in English villages found their way into the towns. We read of
a Shrove Tuesday[1] celebration in London in which, after a morning
spent at cockfighting, "all the youth of the city goes out into the
fields to a much-frequented game of ball. The scholars of each
school have their own ball, and almost all the workers of each trade
have theirs also in their hands. Elder men and fathers and rich citizens come on horseback to watch the contests of their juniors, and
after their fashion are young again with the young."[2] By the mid-
sixteenth century in Cambridge, secularization of the university
notwithstanding, such festive interaction between the town and the
country, between scholar and worker, indeed, between the young
and the old, was, in accordance with official statutes, essentially absent. Each monarch from Henry II forward was obliged to reassert
the "privileged" status of the scholar that protected him from civil
laws and subjected him instead to the strict codes of the university.
This enforced separation of the academic from the civil world is a
good place to begin a discussion of the similarities between the student's and the pastoralist's campus.

"The first condition of pastoral poetry," Frank Kermode tells us,
"is that there should be a sharp difference between two ways of life,
the rustic and the urban" (14). Kermode then makes an interesting
observation that helps to justify his contention that pastoral poetry
stems from nostalgia. Pastoral, he asserts, is essentially an urban
product, produced by poets residing in the city. "The city is an artificial product, and the pastoral poet invariably lives in it, or is the
product of its schools and universities" (14). Two things are implied in this statement. First, that the schools and universities are

38

also "artificial products" and second, that the pastoral poet, though residing in the city, presumably has some recollection of the country. My own assertion, of course, is that Cambridge University is the "artificial product" from which come the meadows and rivers of the poetry I am treating.

The idea that the pastoral worlds of Spenser's, Fletcher's, and Milton's poetry could stem from a reimagined Cambridge world comes largely from readily apparent affinities of the two worlds: they are both worlds of beautiful physical environs set apart from the real (urban, courtly) world, and both are peopled for the most part by youthful men. Consideration of these two obvious traits, along with other ingredients fundamental to both the Arcadian and collegiate worlds, will be the concern of this chapter. Calling Arcadia "the paradise of poetry," Peter Marinelli observes that "it is a middle country of the imagination, half way between a past perfection and a present imperfection, a place of Becoming rather than Being, where an individual's potencies for the arts of life and love and poetry are explored and tested" (37). The "middle country" of pastoral, I suggest, is that space between childhood, "past perfection," and the full adulthood of city and court, "present imperfection."

Marinelli points out, as others have, that the pastoral world is a sort of microcosm of "the greater world," where everyday troubles are magnified as under glass (73). In a certain sense this is true. We see ecclesiastical disputes and complaining in *The Shepheardes Calender* and in "Lycidas." Academic politics fill the *Piscatorie Eclogues*. The troubled love complaints of Colin and others even become everyday by virtue of their repetition. Clearly, the troubles of the poet's world are given voice in the shepherd's songs. The anonymous author of the introduction to the 1771 edition of Fletcher's *Eclogues* reminds his readers that to think, like Joseph Addison, that the only calamities in the pastoral world are a shepherd's foot being pricked by a thorn, a broken crook, or the loss of a favorite lamb is to naively and unnecessarily devalue pastoral poetry. Rather, as this same anonymous author points out, "The complaints of Virgil's Meliboeus will affect every reader because they are real, and come home to every man's concerns" (iii–iv). Even so, as Hobbinol reminds Colin, and as his mere presence reminds us, the pastoral world is not "the greater world." There is nothing everyday about "the pierlesse pleasures" of his "place."

The university world of the Renaissance was just such a "place":

of "the greater world" (an "artificial product" of it), but not in it; part of academic, ecclesiastical, and court politics, but capable of "pierlesse pleasures" that transcended them. This dual status is apparent in the absolute physical separation that the university enjoyed from the rest of the world. For, though a product of the greater world, it was clearly a place apart, as John Venn noted: "It must be remembered that in that day and long afterwards—as we can see in Loggan's maps of 1680—there was hardly anything but open ground—"the fields" as they were called—for many miles round Cambridge: and the limitless marshes were close at hand" (*Early Collegiate Life*, 125). "Lonely and isolated" are words Alexander Judson uses to describe this early Cambridge: "On the north lay the vast, unreclaimed district of the Fens, reedy, wooded, or productive of coarse grass, intersected by numberless watercourses and supporting rude fen-dwellers" (24).

This physical separateness was, of course, an intentional rather than accidental part of the university's composition, and all of the laws of the university reinforced the isolation of the college world from the world beyond. A royal mandate to the sheriff of Cambridge in 1305 repeats "at the request of the masters and scholars Henry III's prohibition on jousts, tournaments and hastiludia in Cambridge or within five miles of it" (Owen, 4). The Cambridge student's education was to be a cloistered one. We know, for example, that students were prohibited not only from residing outside of the colleges in the townsmen's houses,[3] but from attending public performances[4] or even loitering in the town. A 1595 ordinance declares "That no students do walke upon the Market Hill or sitt upon the Stalls or other places thereabout, or make any stay at all in ye said Market place or else where within ye Town, longer then they shall have necessary cause, being appointed by their Tutors to dispatch some necessary business" (Cooper and Cooper, *Annals*, 2.539). Referring to the punishments that might be enforced upon a disobedient student of the time, Venn tell us that it would be redundant and ineffective to "gate" him (prohibit him from going beyond the college grounds), "for the entire college was then in the present sense of the term, permanently gated" (113).

By the time Milton arrived at Cambridge in 1625, some growth had taken place; the population of the town may have been as much as nine thousand (Masson, 115). Still, separation from the world remained the natural as well as the ideological circumstance of Cambridge: "Then, as now," Masson tells us in his *Life of Milton*, "the distinction between 'town' and 'gown' was one of the fixed ideas of the place" (115). "They are the sun," Dr. Caius declared of sixteenth-century students, "and the townsmen are mere darkness" (Gray, 14). The following passage from Masson describes well the layers of cloister between the greater world and the student: "Into the little world of Christ's College . . . forming a community by itself . . . of some two hundred and fifty persons, and surrounded again by that larger world of the total University to which it was related as a part, we are to fancy Milton introduced in the month of February 1625" (131).

Descriptions of the university world by Masson or Judson typically include enthusiastic depictions of the architecture. What is assumed is the natural beauty of the surroundings. Much is implicit within words like fields and grounds, and while the Cambridge of the early seventeenth century may not have been the place that Hobbinol describes in the June Eclogue of the *Calender*, it was likely a pleasant "orchard" where the young Ridley "learned without book almost all of Paul's epistles, as the walls, butts and trees, if they could speak, might bear witness" (Gray, 145–46). We read of one "Joh Carowe," who in 1593 was accorded privileges as "Academic gardener" (University Registry Guard Books in Cambridge University Archives [hereinafter cited as U.A.], CUR 11.12.27). And the following admonition is contained in an ordinance, written in 1570, for the protection of willow trees: "And if any person or persons shall at any time or times hereafter cut down, saw or hew, pluck up by the root, bark, spoil or destroy, any willow or willows now set or hereafter set, in any part of the bounds or commons of this town, that then every such offender shall suffer pains, forfeitures and losses, as the common laws of this realm shall appoint or assign" (Cooper and Cooper, 2.157). The particular motives for making sacred this most elegiac of trees are not certain. Presumably the rationale was more horticultural than literary, but the implicit Ardenic declaration that one will suffer pains and losses for carving in the bark of a willow tree offers us a provocative glimpse, not just of the beauty of the natural surroundings of Cambridge, but also of the priorities of those governing this environment.

Ironically, the creation of college gardens frequently took place by the enclosure of what had been public land. Many disturbances arose at these times between the university and Cambridge townspeople, as well as local farmers and shepherds. At an insurrection in 1552 citizens made the following complaints:

It. We fynde that Trinitie College hath inclosed a common lane which
was a common course both for cart and horse and man leadinge to the
ryver unto a common grene and no recompense made therefore.
It. We fynde that the seyde College dothe commonlye ust to laye ther
mucke and meanor on the back syde apon the foreseyde common grene
wher thei wyll suffer no man ells to do the lyke and have builded a
common Jake apon part of the same. (Lamb, 158)

In response to these and dozens of other complaints, an anonymous
poet—in all probability a university wit—composed a satirical pastoral ballad whose title relies upon the familiar slang use of Jake/
Jack/John for toilet and quibbles "style" for sty, arriving at: "Jake
of the Northe Beyonde the Style Speaketh," that is, "The Toilet
North of the Sty Speaks." Herein individual shepherds register their
complaints to a consoling Jake of the Northe.

(Incidentally and interestingly, doggerel though it is, this ballad
may have helped inspire John Skelton's adopted persona, which
eventually became the latter part of Edmund Spenser's pastoral
pseudonym. Having chosen Colin from his classical ancestry, he
and Skelton found their literary surname more locally. In Jake's
ballad, Jake's pastoral "cousins" Robbyn and Harry Clowte each
speak a versed complaint. The yoking of the Virgilian Colin with
the rural English Clout is a yoking of the mythical and the actual:
the very name Colin Clout contains Spenser's literary inspiration as
well as a more immediate, if not, perhaps, so inspiring, source for
his pastoral poetry.)

The separation from the greater world that a pseudo-Clout like
Edmund Spenser enjoyed within the world of the university is one
important characteristic that connects this world to versions of Arcadia. A second one, which bears mentioning before exploring
more specific connections, is the predominant population of youth
in both worlds. "The first fact to be impressed on the mind is the
extreme youth of the ordinary student, or rather the junior portion
of the students. In the sixteenth and seventeenth centuries the 'lad'
was seldom more than 16, and often under 15 or even 14, at admis-
sion; and he very frequently resided for six or seven years" (Venn,
112). Milton was sixteen upon coming to Cambridge, Fletcher was
eighteen, and Spenser, seventeen. Youth itself, while not always
blissful, lends itself to all sorts of joys, the underlying one being
the joy of making new discoveries and formulating new percep-
tions. Such discoveries and formulations supply much of the subject matter for pastoral songs.

Like the singers in the pastoral world, the residents of the university world are young enough to seek the joys that life has newly offered them. Poggioli claims that "adolescence and early adulthood are the only important pastoral ages since they coincide with the mating seasons of human life" (57). Love, however, is but one of the joys for which the student/swain is at a ripe age. Youth itself, in fact, is a pastoral joy, and not just in the case of the Pastoral of Love, but in the Pastoral of Innocence as well. For adolescence and early adulthood are ages, not just of sexual discovery, but of many discoveries, both political and nonpolitical. The resulting changes in perception and the formulation of new perspectives occurs ideally, not amidst the fog of sexual awakening, but within the more reliable framework provided by platonic fellowship.

COLLEGIATE FELLOWSHIP

Out of Virgilian pastoral come two essential ingredients for pastoral happiness: "first a thorough understanding of the workings of the universe; and second, a life of simple good fellowship, with a company of like-minded and unambitious friends" (Rosenmeyer, 66). Both of these ingredients were fundamental as well to the academic world of sixteenth- and seventeenth-century England: an understanding of the universe being the common pursuit, and the fellowship of unambitious friends providing the ideal circumstance for that pursuit. Such lofty sights and circumstance, like the common clothing and language of the pastoral world, while explicitly anti-court, were certainly not anti-university. Fellowship, in fact, was the central ingredient of both the pastoral *campus* and the university campus. Neither the swain nor the student was alone in his world, nor in his understanding of the world.

As freedom in the pastoral world is dependent upon a circle of friends, freedom within the university world was likewise so. Peaceful association with one's peers was as much a necessity as a privilege for both swain and student, as is evidenced in the plight of Gabriel Harvey, refused supplicant for his degree of Master of Arts because "he was not familiar like a fellow and did disdain every man's company." The members of Pembroke College complained of Harvey that he "needs in al hast be studdiing in Christmas, when other were plaiing and was when whottest at mi book when the rest were hardist at their cards" (Attwater, 45). Harvey, whose degree was eventually granted by the intervention of Master Young, claimed for his part "that at usual and convenient times, as after dinner and supper, and commenti fiers, yea and at other times too, if the lest occasion were offrid, I continued as ani and was as fellowi at the best. What thai call sociable I know not: this I am suer, I never avoided cumpani: I have bene merri in cumpani: I have bene ful hardly drawn out of cumpani" (Attwater, 45). This example illustrates how much was to be gained or lost by the company of one's peers. A circle of the right friends yielded not only the benefit of company but also, perhaps, advancement. As in the court, students with political or literary aspirations would aid themselves by being part of a particular clique.

One reason for Harvey's purported lack of sociability, in fact, may be due to the value he placed upon more private friendships with the likes of Edmund Spenser. Making a convincing case that Spenser and Gabriel Harvey conspired together to create a fictive Harvey-Spenser construct in the *Calender*'s E. K., Louise Schleiner claims that "an idealized Kent is clearly the *Calender*'s mental locale" (383). And while my present argument neither rests nor insists upon her claim, it is one with which my own evidence concurs, albeit with the following important exception. The academic ingame that Schleiner describes between "Edmund of Kent" and "Aulus Pembrochianus Socius" belongs, not to the countryside of Kent, but to the already idealized locus of Pembroke College, where the two men had resided together, where the rules for such games were developed, and where Spenser, under the tutelage of Harvey, acquired his "sundry studies and laudable partes of learning wherein how or Poete is seene, be they witnesse which are privie to his study" (December Glosse). Such a private conspiracy of song-making finds its parallel in the pastoral world, where small groups of shepherds gather to hear and evaluate one another's songs. Where the concern is "pastoral song," or literary competition, such as that between Harvey and Spenser, or between Tompkins and Fletcher, the atmosphere is, ideally, like that of the shepherd's singing matches, which conclude in mutual admiration. Such rivalry enhances rather than destroys fellowship.

Eventually, these circles of companions within the university began to directly mimic the pastoral poems that they inspired. During Fletcher's years at Cambridge, Abram Langdale observes that "the Cambridge society of poets surrounded Fletcher and celebrated him as their president. This clique was founded in accordance with the traditional laws of the pastoral cult" (46). In using pastoral laws to form their group, these students quite deliberately shaped their lives to imitate art. In Fletcher's *Eclogues*, art returns the compliment. Such "pastoral" cliques as these usually had at their center one more prominent poet around whom the rest of the group gathered.[5] The size of such a group ranged from two to perhaps as many as six or seven, but ultimately we find, in and out of the *amoebeans* [singing contests], that in nearly all pastoral eclogues the pastoral number is two. Pastoral is largely composed of the often intimate, sometimes hostile, exchange between two swains. Such dialogues in the poetry of Spenser, Fletcher, and Milton can be traced to Cambridge friendships.

Of these friendships and others that these men had, we probably know the most about that of Fletcher and Tompkins, which serves as an excellent example of a Cambridge friendship turned into pastoral poetry. According to Langdale: "Tompkins shared the poet's inmost thoughts, became the confidant of his love affairs and his consolation in disappointment. . . . The relationship was all the more vital because it was concentrated within Fletcher's creative years and colored nearly all of his major works" (44). The intimacy between these two men is not only the subject of Fletcher's Eclogue VI, but, like the relationship of Colin to Hobbinol in *The Shepheardes Calender*, it governs the *Eclogues* as a whole. "I love my health, my life, my books, my friends, / Thee (dearest Thomalin) Nothing above thee" ("To Thomalin"), expresses the essence of pastoral friendship, especially insofar as it exceeds the "true love" between swain and maiden, as Thirsil insists that it does.

The university conversations in which these poets' fraternal friendships were formed were not free of governing rules. Students' conversations with one another, except in their chambers or during the hours of relaxation, were restricted to Latin, Greek, or Hebrew,[6] an inhibition indeed even for the most learned students. The bedchamber, then, was one refuge within the university where the student was allowed to converse freely in his native tongue. It was unusual during these times for a member of a college to have a chamber wholly to himself. Two or three students usually shared the same room, and consequently, we read in the college biographies of the time "of the chum or chamber-fellow of the hero as either assisting or retarding his conversation" (Masson, 133). The very fact that conversation is thus described emphasizes its importance.

We know of course that students, by whatever means, managed

to converse in English outside of their bedchambers. We read of walks in the garden, through the town at night, and in the surrounding fields and woods. Such excursions were not likely to have been illuminated by Latin discourses, nor was the content of such common English conversations restricted, as would be the mandatory Latin conversing that took place in the halls of the university. The requirement of Latin conversations was intended to limit the participants to elevated scholarly discourse. Students undoubtedly looked forward to excursions and to the bedchamber in order to talk in English about love, poetry, and politics. As such talk was not likely to go unpunished, the more private the milieu, the better. Take, for example, the case of one Richard Nichols, reprimanded in the early seventeenth century "for sitting up all night in a tavern and advancing several things in favour of Popery" (U.A., CUR 4.11), or this complaint against T. Synth, Fellow of Christ's, for "attacking in a common place, the surplice, the Crofs, the churching of women, Burial with Prayer" (U.A., CUR 4.24.1). Students undoubtedly sought less public, if not less inebriating, contexts in which to discourse freely on such matters in their native tongue. Given the freedom to speak freely, we can be sure that they did precisely that, and that the tone and substance of such conversations were as common, they might say as "base," as English itself.

We begin to sense here the significance of, first Spenser, and then the others, writing their pastorals in vernacular English. A more traditional following of Virgil—indeed, a more courtly following—would have been composed in formal Latin or French, and Spenser was certainly capable of this task. One reason for the choice of English, of course, was its commonness. Being the common tongue, it served as the language of the "common" Clout. Spenser even chose to embellish his pastorals with a pseudo-antiquated communality. Yet there is more here than just the desire to portray commonness. In the above circumstances, English, for the university student, would also denote privacy. Thus, English was not just the more common tongue but the more intimate. Being rustics, Spenser's swains speak in a common rustic tongue, but common only to themselves. In his choice of English over Latin, Spenser clearly conceived of the pastoral genre as linguistically intimate, and used it accordingly.

As the more common tongue, English lends itself to conversing on the common matters of the shepherd's or fisherman's trade. As the more intimate tongue, English allows for, perhaps actually invites, conversing on personal matters of the swains' hearts. With regard to content, the conversations in the *Shepheardes Calender* are essentially like those that took place in the Cambridge gardens and bedchambers—implicitly intimate, fraternal exchanges between two youths. They praise one another's songs, "O Colin, Colin, the shepheards joye, / How I admire ech turning of thy verse" (August, 192–93); reveal their private ambitions, "Piers, I have pyped erst so long with payne, / That all mine Oten reedes bene rent and wore: / And my poore Muse hath spent her spared store, / Yet little good hath got, and much less gayne" (October, 7–10); engage in ecclesiastical debate, "Syker, thous but a laesie loord, / and rekes much of thy swinck, / That with fond termes, and eetlesse words / to blere myne eyes doest thinke" (July, 33–36); "make purpose of love and other pleasuance," (March, Argument); and pass along gossip, "Colin thou kenst, the Southerne shepheardes boye: / Him love hath wounded with a deadly darte" (April, 21–22).

From Theocritus on, this pastoral pleasure of conversation comes intertwined with a bucolic setting, a pleasant place. Apart from the college gardens themselves, a makeshift version of such a locus would have been afforded by the countryside surrounding Cambridge.[7] The inconvenience of arranging bucolic conversations no doubt heightened their pleasure, and their inevitable occurence furnishes a direct and richly suggestive connection between the life of the academic world and the subsequent pastoral poetry of a student like Spenser, for whom the country may have been a locus of fellowship and learning.

Likewise, students' vacations from the university often took the form of bucolic retreat. Charles Gawdy, for example, writing to his father in 1637, requests payment to his tutor for "that quarter when I was in the countrie" (Venn, 229). In the following undated letter written from Oxfordian Diodati to his friend John Milton, we see why such bucolic ventures, in and of themselves, are not necessarily pastoral:

> I have no fault to find with my present mode of life, except this alone, that I lack some kindred spirit that can give and take with me in conversation. For such I long; but all other enjoyments are abundant here in the country; for what more is wanting when the days are long, the scenery blooming beautifully with flowers, and waving and teeming with leaves, on every branch a nightingale or goldfinch or other small bird glorying

in its songs and warblings, most varied walks, a table neither scant nor overloaded, and sleep undisturbed. If I could provide myself in addition with a good companion, I mean an educated one and initiated in the mysteries, I should be happier than the King of the Persians. (Masson, 163)

Here is Epicurean bliss without the Epicurean companion. The setting is every bit the *locus amoenus*—the table bears the fruits of moderation, no worry harasses his sleep, and yet, left alone, Diodati lacks the essential ingredient of pastoral: companionship. The Oxford student sounds here much like Hobbinol in the June Eclogue of the *Calender* who, like Diodati, lacks only the good conversation formerly provided him by his companion. Diodati has found a place for song, but there is no one to hear him sing. Note as well that for Diodati as well as for Hobbinol, Thomalin, and the uncouth swain of "Lycidas," not just any companion will do. He requires "an educated one . . . initiated in the mysteries," one presumably with whom he can share not just conversation, but verse.

COLLEGIATE LOVE

These friendships of Spenser, Milton, and Fletcher were based chiefly on "the mysteries" of poetry, just as the pastoral dialogues of their eclogues concerned the common activity of composing and singing songs. The subject of the songs themselves is often True Love, which, by necessity, brought both the Cambridge student and the pastoral swain beyond the boundaried world that they inhabited, as the university world was even more insistent than the pastoral in its prohibition of the women, its reason being chiefly religious as well as a further extension of the official town and gown division.

As early as 1459, royal letters renewed university powers "to expel prostitutes and lewd women to a distance of at least four miles from Cambridge" (Owen, 13). That this prohibition was taken seriously is evidenced by the imprisonment of W. Austen and Ds. R. Elain of St. John's for assisting one such prostitute on 18 September 1592 or 1593 (U.A., CUR 16.2). The convent of Barnwell, well within the proscribed four-mile circumference, was, predictably, a well-known place to Cambridge University residents. In 1566 an allegation was made against T. Longwourth "for defamation by reporting that he kept a woman at Barnwell" (U.A., CUR

4.22). In April of 1594, Ds. Glanville was "degraded and imprisoned for a riot at Barnwell" (U.A., CUR 16.3). That many other allegations of fornication and adultery (Brigitt, wife of J. Edwards, M.A., 1596) accompany these entries is not surprising, but what is perhaps surprising are the number of "paternity suits" against fellows and masters at Cambridge at this time, two examples being Agnes Linsey's allegation "laid to roger Andrews, M.A., Fellow of Pembroke, 29 July, 1598" (U.A., CUR 4.24) and Mary Cattle's penance for having a bastard by Kantnile Legg, the supposed father, on 29 September 1595 (U.A., CUR 11.20.1).

An injunction issued in 1630 by King Charles I suggests that marriage had become a way to confound both charges of fornication and paternity charges. The injunction declares that: "no scholar marry a townswoman under pain of degradation and expulsion without consent of his parents and tutors: that no woman be employed in college but as nurses—that no nurse . . . be under 50 and that they never send their daughters or maids to college chambers" (U.A., CUR 13.21). Like speaking in one's native tongue, sex is, of course, not something to be prevented by royal injunction. Nonetheless, the efforts to keep the college student separate from the mysteries of love, like the prohibitions against speaking in English, only increase love's remoteness and thus the sufferer's fancy. Such prohibition thereby furnishes a rich connection between the scholastic and the pastoral world.

Though opinions vary concerning the role that love plays in the pastoral world, it seems clear that this world, like that of the Renaissance university, is essentially a man's world. Just as women were prohibited from the cloistered academic campus, so they are virtually absent from the shepherd's world in English poetry. Renato Poggioli claimed that English poets so developed the pastoral of innocence that they neglected the pastoral of love and happiness that would fulfill the passion of love and erotic wishes (58). Made "Petrarchan" by collegiate circumstance, it is little wonder that these poets' shepherds should likewise be so. Lack of fulfillment typifies the pastorals I am considering. They contain plenty of love laments, but all passion goes unrequited. Lack of consummation, in fact, is what propels these pastorals forward, what gives the swains something to pipe about. As Rosenmeyer describes it, love is an animating force that enlivens *otium*. If successful, it would be higher than *otium*. If unsuccessful, it would destroy *otium*. The naturalness of love, Rosenmeyer asserts, is tempered by its lack of consummation (85).

What compensates for unconsummated love affairs in both campuses is the consummation of actual friendships, which is why pastoral fellowship, and not true love, is the central joy in the world of both student and swain. The loves of whom the swains sing in their pastorals, while not imaginary, are, at best, beautiful objects. Colin's lovesickness takes up a good part of the *Calender*. Even so, we learn little of the object of his affection other than that she is "a countrie lasse called Rosalinde" who cares very little either for him or his piping. In Eclogue III of the *Piscatorie Eclogues*, Myrtil suffers love's madness when "A friendly fisher brought the boy to view / Coelia the fair." (St. 2, 1.2–3) Though in such matters there is no consolation, the "swowning" Myrtil is at least kept alive and comforted by his friends: "Till fisher-boyes (fond fisher-boyes) revive him, / And back again his life and loving give him" (3.20, l. 2–3).

The objects of the shepherds' affections exist, like those of the university student, beyond the boundary of the campus (in Colin's case, for example, in the neighboring town). The consummation of such a love requires that the lover—be he student or swain—go beyond the boundaries of the pastoral circle (at least four miles in the case of the Cambridge student). If successful, this lover will find a love that replaces *otium*. The very pondering of true love, therefore, while it enlivens *otium*, simultaneously threatens the destruction of the pastoral circle. Thus, Hobbinol (about whom we learn much more than Rosalind) can, like the Harvey whom he represents, rail against romantic love for more than just reasons of principle. Such love is not only immoderate, unrealistic, and, therefore, the source of inevitable misery, it also threatens the pastoral circle. Colin not only scorns Hobbinol's gifts, he hands them over to a woman who scorns pastoral song: "Shepheardes device she hateth as the snake." This comparison of Colin's pipe to the familiar phallic reptile that disrupted Eden would seem to belong to Rosalind herself. In reporting it, Hobbinol not only invokes the memory of the original lost garden, but enjoys some clever sexual humor at Colin's expense. Rosalind, he tells us, rejects Colin's musical as well as his peculiarly masculine device, his song as well as what she rightly perceives to be his reason for singing—his sexual desire for her. This very desire is what has jeopardized the preexisting love between himself and Hobbinol, and his clever complaint continues:

"The ladde, whome long I lovd so deare, / Nowe loves a lasse."
Hobbinol's quibbling here equates woman ("a lasse") with a sigh
of futility ("alas"), perhaps the most compressed argument ever
made on the transience of romantic love. Ironically, however, for
all of Hobbinol's cleverness, Colin's eventual departure from the
world of the *Calender* is itself an eloquent argument on the transience and unreality of pastoral *otium*.

In Eclogue VI of Fletcher's *Eclogues* the lovesickness of Thomalin comes between himself and Thirsil. Thirsil, not as easily put
off as Hobbinol is by Colin, challenges his friend:

> Thomalin, I see thy Thirsil thou neglect'st
> Some greater love holds down thy heart in fear;
> Thy Thirsils love, and counsel thou reject'st;
> Thy soul was wont to lodge within my eare:
> But now that port no longer thou respect'st;
> Yet hath it still been safely harbour'd there.
>
> (VI.l.1–6)

We see here the critical importance of conversation to the pastoral
friendship, which is formed by the lodging of one's soul in another's ear. The college world, far more so than the world of the court,
provided the occasion for such an intimate lodging. When Thirsil
extracts a confession from Thomalin, he discovers that it is the
nymph, Sweet Melite, who is behind the neglect of the friendship.
Thirsil does not regard his friend's recent infatuation with the
nymph as a "greater love." For though he too once had his heart
held down in fear, he is now cured, and uses his own experience to
persuade Thomalin of a love higher than that which wounds:
"Those storms of looser fire are laid low; / And higher love safe
anchors in my heart: / So now a quiet calm does safely reigne"
(17.l.1–7). This quiet calm, this *otium*, requires that Thomalin be
unbound from his love of Melite, who has left him with a captive
heart. Thirsil tells him that "If from this love thy will thou canst
unbinde" (26.l.3), proper pastoral freedom can be restored: "To
morrow shall we feast; then hand in hand / Free will we sing, and
dance along the golden sand" (26.l.8–9).

This freedom is the same fraternal freedom not merely allowed
in the university but, in a sense, required. Being wounded by Rosal-
indes or Melites meant that the student must venture not just beyond his own pastoral circle, but beyond the cloistering walls of the

all-male university environment. In Langdale we read of Fletcher's trips from Cambridge to visit his cousins, where he enjoyed at least one courtship. Judson suggests that, since Colin represents Spenser, love may have been the "exciting force" that prompted Spenser's departure from Cambridge.[8] In the real world, as in the pastoral world, the consummation of love often meant marriage and maturity. It is less the loss of youth, perhaps, than the coming of age. Call it what we wish, it is essentially the death of the pastoral circle and the loss of the freedom that circle represents. For marriage is the institution of a civilized society apart from the pastoral world. It belongs at the court, not on the campus,[9] and, like the court, it is something to which the student aspires only after departing from the campus.

COLLEGIATE RIVALRY

Like fellowship, the joy of rivalry was an ingredient that the English pastoralists found both in their classical models and in their immediate university environs. The rivalry in the pastorals of Theocritus and Virgil takes the form of singing matches between two rival swains who exchange boasts, usually about their respective beloveds. These matches are usually friendly exchanges that end in mutual admiration and gift-giving, although sometimes they are less than friendly bouts that must be resolved by an intervening third party. In either case, the contests provide the excuse—the frame—for pastoral songs, and at the same time illustrate the pastoral joy that is as much a part of the pastoral world as singing itself: the joy of competitive rivalry. The sport and rivalry that, in English pastoral, we find contained mostly within singing matches, was, in earlier poetry, more varied, and often more physical.

In the fourth of Theocritus's idylls, for example, Corydon tells Battus that the goatherd Aegon has been carried off to Alpheus because "Men say he rivals Heracles in might" (l.8). In the fifth idyll a goatherd and a shepherd precede their piping with accusations of theft, and then venture into progressively cruder subject matter before arriving at this final exchange before the singing match:

> *Comatas.* Most excellent blockhead, all I say, I, is true, though for my part I'm no braggart; but Lord! what a railer is here!

Lacon.   Come, come; say thy say and be done, and let's suffer friend Morson to come off with his life. Apollo save us, Comatas! thou hast the gift o' the gab.

(1.76–79)

Such "gift o' the gab" is weeded out by Virgil in order to make room for more refined song. The shepherds have less to do with sheep and more to do with singing, and along with the bantering and song go also suggestions of Herculean strength and physical prouess. In Spenser the conversations are resumed, but this time in a decidedly collegiate manner. Thenot and Cuddie rival as old and young; Piers and Palinode dispute as churchmen, but in the other eclogues of the *Calender* rivalry has been largely replaced by collegiality. The eclogues are governed by "arguments" and the swains typically give more energy to conversation than song. Spenser reserves the more raucus Theocritan rivalry for Book VI of *The Faerie Queene*, where the shepherds, "To practise games, and maistcries to try" (9.43.6), turn to wrestling. Such physical contests have no place in the "arguments" of *The Shepheards Calender*. When we compare it with its classical models, we see that the English pastoral was clearly born more of the classroom than the country.

That *campus* meant originally "field of contest" gives us a good idea of the sorts of pastoral play to be found in the world of the university. Pastoral rivalry found a place in the dormitory, the lecture hall, the playing field, and, in its most mischievous form, beyond the campus. The rivalry and sport of the university world took basically two forms, legal and illegal, with a clear and unsurprising preference being shown for the latter. The result, in both the world of the university and that of the English pastoral, was a perpetual tension between Epicurean impulses and puritanical restraint, a tension that in both worlds resulted inevitably in a rivalry between youth and age. This rivalry gives way to debate. For in neither the pastoral nor the university world do the impulses of youth go unchecked by age. Elder shepherds reside in the pastoral, just as in the university there are elder tutors, and in both cases it is the duty of these elders to instruct. Often, be they shepherd or tutor, the subject of their instruction is "the greater world" to which they have gone and in which they have lived, and from which they have returned wiser.[10] Those whom they instruct, however, by the virtue of their youth and numbers, are the proprietors of this world of youthful joys.

In *The Shepheardes Calender*, Thenot and Piers know the maturity of age, the brevity of life, and the empty promises of the greater world. They advocate a puritanical restraint that is lost on Cuddie and Hobbinol, who, in harmony with the *locus amoenus*, are true pastoral shepherds,[11] enjoying the delights of youth to which Colin bids a reluctant adieu.

This continual, pastoral tension between Epicurean impulses and puritanical restraint had its corollary in the world of Cambridge University, where, as in the pastoral world, the proprietors were the young. In his description of undergraduate life in the sixteenth century, John Venn suggests that the impulse toward disobedience was rather a way of life. Speculating where one might find a Cambridge student of that day, Venn writes: "If he was forbidden to attend bull-baitings, to go fowling in Chesterton marshes, or to bathe in the river [Cam], we gain a clue as to where we should be likely to find him of a summer's afternoon" (111–12). Students were likewise prohibited from such pastoral play as bowling and "Nine hoals, or such like unlawful games." The same list of prohibitions printed in 1595 orders "that the hurtfull and unscholarlike exercise of Football and meetings tending to that end, do from henceforth utterly cease (except within places severall to ye Colledges, and that for them only that be of ye same Colledges" (Cooper and Cooper, 2.538–39). Such prohibitions, it would seem, gave students ample opportunity for disobedience.

The rivalry between colleges, which the above prohibition on football seeks to suppress, is, of course, legendary, one of the most famous being between St. John's and Trinity Colleges. In February of 1610 we find a "Complaint of the Fellows and Scholars of St. John's against the stage keepers at Trinity for making a riot, alarming and wounding many at the last 2 comedies" (U.A., CUR 93.9). Having warned the members of St. John's not to attend comedies being performed at Trinity, the members of Trinity College then fortified themselves within their tower with buckets of water and an ample supply of stones, which they proceeded to unload upon the visitors from the rival college. "Pratt of St. John's, standing facing Trinity by the trompeters, received a grievous wound from a stone cast from the Tower." (Cooper and Cooper, 2.601). University manuscripts are likewise littered with various complaints of and punishments for students brawling with one another.

Tired of such diversion, one could always venture beyond the college walls, upon some excuse or another, where awaited the perpetual quarrel between town and gown. In a letter of 1563, William Soone describes Cambridge students carousing through the streets of town "perpetually quarreling and fighting" with the townsfolk: "They go out in the night to show their valour, armed with monstrous great clubs furnished with a cross piece of iron to keep off the blows,[12] and frequently beat the watch." Like romantic love, the violence of arms was reserved for ventures beyond the safe and prohibitive confines of the collegiate cloister. Concerning such nighttime recreation, Soone concludes: "the way of life in these colleges is the most pleasant and liberal: and if I might have my choice, and my principles would permit, I should prefer it to a kingdom."[13]

The pleasantness to which Soone refers is that which happens in spite of, and not because of, the burdensome university codes that one might defy by going "unto . . . victualling Houses and Taverns," eating flesh on Fridays, missing prayers, or simply being in disorderly dress. In 1600, Ds. Pepper of Corpus Christi, "for being present at certain interludes without his habit and in unseemly dress [was] ordered out of court where his hair [was] pulled immediately" (U.A., CUR 16.6). Upset by students wearing "ye new fashioned gowns of any color whatsoever, blew or green or red or mixt" (Cooper and Cooper, 3.280), a Cambridge authority in the late-sixteenth century declared that: "if remedy be not speedely provyded, the University, which hath bene from the begyning a collection and society of a multitude of all sorts of ages, and professyng to godlines, modesty, vertew, and lerning, and a necesary storehouse to the realme of the same, shall become rather a storehouse for a stable of prodigall wastfull ryotous, unlerned and insufficient persons" (Cooper and Cooper, 2.361). A nearly identical complaint is delivered by Piers, the shepherd-guardian, in May of *The Shepheardes Calender*; when informed by his more liberal companion, Palinode, that "Yougthes folke now flocken in euery where / To gather may buskets and smelling brere" (l.9–10), Piers responds:

> Perdie so farre am I from enuie,
> That their fondnesse inly I pitie.
> Those faytours little regarden their charge,
> While they letting their sheepe runne at large,
> Passen their time, that should be sparely spent,
> In lustehede and wanton meryment.

(l.37–42)

For Piers, the shepherd is Shepherd—that is, a proper Christian minister. He has no envy for the Epicurean joys, gratuitous interests, and leisurely activities described by Palinode. He, with Bishop Gardiner addressing university masters in 1530, understands "How necessary it is to brydle the arrogance of youngest" (Lamb, 45).

Unfortunately for both Piers and the Cambridge authorities, wanton merriment would not subside, and the Epicurean impulses that are the joy of the pastoral world would prevail over the puritanical codes that governed the university. Eclogue IV of Fletcher's *Piscatorie Eclogues* records this decline in discipline at Cambridge University. As fisher Thelgon (an allegorical figure for Fletcher's own father), departs Chamus's shores, he laments the deterioration of the fishers' trade, and complains that his songs will be replaced by the songs of "a crue of idle grooms, / Idle and bold that never saw the seas" (14.1–2). Such as these, he tells Chromis, will fill the empty rooms and enjoy lazy living and "bathing in wealth and ease" (14.3–4)—bathing, too, no doubt, in the River Cam, come the month of May.

Despite the frolic of the students on the sporting fields, in the river and woods, and through the dark streets of town, the rivalries that occupied them most occurred in the corridors of the university—namely, the rivalry of minds. As Victor Morgan observes, "conflicts between different colleges were also occasioned by the public disputations that were part of the academic curriculum at both Oxford and Cambridge. . . . The possibility of these conflicts occurring became more likely as the antagonisms increased between the Calvinist and the Arminian parties within the Universities" (188). This rivalry was played out in conversations fed by murmured rumor that raised up some and lowered others, in a never-ending parade of academic and ecclesiastical disputes, nourished and intensified by the changing monarchs and the subsequent "visitations." Thus rumor might carry word of the latest of the attacks on the existing church system by Thomas Cartwright, or news of a rebuttal by Elizabeth's loyalist, John Whitgift. Such events, Judson notes, would not be soon forgotten. "The emotional life of large bodies of young men must find some outlet," he says, "and in the absence of important athletic contests, it probably concerned itself at this time with events such as these" (33).

Rumor might, about this same time, encourage the young fellows of Pembroke Hall not to vote for Gabriel Harvey in his appeal for master of arts. Thus, it is no surprise that, in the covert shades and bowers of the *Calender*, we are privy to more than just the "delectable Theocritan controversy" of who is the best singer of songs. We hear as well talk of who is and is not a worthy shepherd (May, July), how badly love has ruined a fellow swain (Hobbinol's constant theme), and reports of the general wickedness of the world (Diggon's lament in September). As he recounts the university's injustice to his father, Fletcher's eclogues take on a particularly Theocritan tone. Chame, having given to the worthy fisher, Thelgon, a costly boat (i.e., fellowship), then "bequeathed it to a wandring guest" (II.12.3). Thelgon no sooner regains his "boat" when "Chame to Gripus gave it once again, / Gripus, the basest and most dunghill swain / That ever drew a net, or fisht in fruitfull main" (II.14.6–8). By Eclogue IV, Thirsil's own consolation comes from "the Prince of Fishers," who, like Chame, appears again in Milton's "Lycidas" where "Chamus, reverend sire," demands "Ah! who hath reft . . . my dearest pledge" (107) and the pilot of the Galilean Lake rails against "Blind mouths! that scarce themselves know how to hold / A sheep-hook" (120–21).

COLLEGIATE POVERTY

One may observe other academic similarities between the poets' world of Cambridge and the worlds of their subsequent pastoral poems, one such similarity being the practice of poverty that Theocritus calls the "one stirrer-up of the crafts . . . the true teacher of labour" (Idyll 21.1.3). The exchange of funds or currency by which, for instance, one's reputation might be bought or sold at the court, was not a part of the student's world.[14] The delight of poverty for the shepherd is not the aesthetic Christian discipline of chosen austerity but the Epicurean joy of communality. The shepherd shares with his companions common garb and common tasks, in contrast to those at the court, for whom *negotium* has taken the place of *otium*. The Greek equivalent of *otium*, of course, is *scholia*. The scholar's leisure, like that of the shepherd's, derives from his freedom from economic concerns. If not supported by family or patron, the student supported himself with his own labor. Spenser, for example, attended the Merchant Taylor's School as a "poor scholar" and served at Pembroke as a sizar, a student who received lodging and an education in exchange for his services and a nominal fee. As Richard Helgerson notes, "in presenting himself as a shepherd-poet, [Spenser] suffered no major declassment" (896).

Freedom from worldly transactions, combined with the simpler life necessitated by a universally poorer world, allowed for a sort of ideal poverty by which the student could, if he wished, disdain the wealth of the world in the same fashion as the shepherd. Just as he could cast aside his Latin learning in order to adopt the simple tongue of the swain, so too this student of the separate world of the university (and the separate college worlds within the university) could pretend to enjoy the self-sufficiency of a pastoral economy that "equates its desires with its needs and ignores industry and trade; even its barter with the outside world is more an exchange of gifts than of commodities. Money, credit, and debt have no place in an economy of this kind" (Poggioli, 5).

Such a barter with the outside world is the inevitable appeal for funds that the student must make to his patron. The following appeal for funds comes from a letter written by Anthony Gawdy (cousin to Charles) in August of 1626. Gawdy desires to have some new clothes for spring and we see that he does indeed perceive this dealing as an exchange of gifts, rather than commodities. More than that, however, we see in the letter, which he signs "Yor Porre Kinsman," that the imaginative young man fancies himself in a world of nature quite apart from the world of commerce: "I confess it is the time now when nature doeth cloeth all hir cretures: the earth with grase, as the cloeth, and with diversitye of flowers as it were the triming or setting out the garment" (Venn, 197).

Gawdy obviously desires more here than the standard weeds provided him by the university, probably without expense. If the court was made colorful by elaborate costumes, the campus, like the pastoral world, was distinguished by simplicity in dress. The common dress of the Cambridge student was as much clerical as scholarly; it included a gown that reached down to his heels and a sacred cap of the variety worn by priests. The following regulations also applied: "No student shall wear within the university, any hoses of unsemely greatnes or disguised fashion, nor yet any excessyve ruffs in ther shyrts; nor shall any person wear swords or rapiers but when they ar to ryde abroad; nether shall any person come to study, wear any apparell of velvet or silk" (Cooper and Cooper, 2.361). The decree against weaponry is pastoral enough, but, as might be expected, and as is certainly evident from Gawdy's letter, this required uniformity of dress was not in itself a delight. If the students enjoyed the common life, they missed the color and frills of the greater world that nature herself wore quite openly.[15]

Residents of the pastoral world are joined, not just by the "weeds" they wear, but the tasks they perform, tasks which, performed willingly, are not like the drudgery of the work-a-day world, but a fruitful manner of living by which they are freed from the normal curse of work. Generally speaking, the student in his cloistered world had as little to do with the usual curse of work as he did with industry and trade. Like the swain, he enjoyed instead a sort of *hesychia*, or work without toil. We find decrees such as the following one made by the vice-chancellor of Cambridge in 1570, to be rather an exception: "No inhabitant within the town of Cambridge, being scholar or scholars servant, can or may be privileged by that title, from the common days work of mending the highways" (Cooper and Cooper, 2.250). The very fact that such a decree had to be made indicates that there was much from which the scholar, by virtue of his privileged status, was exempt, including imprisonment and legal suits.[16] In any case, we can be sure that study, not roadwork, was the chief occupation of the Cambridge scholar. The common task of learning, requiring as it does *scholia*, *otium*, links the university student to the pastoral swain, whose only real tool is an oaten pipe. The private ponderings, learned conversations, formal debates, and verse composition in which the students spent their days were tasks like the "work" of the shepherd and fisher swains, whose primary occupation was neither herding nor fishing, but singing. The infringement of municipal laws and labor—like the black plague itself—threatened the potential *otium* of the academic cloister.

COLLEGIATE INHERITANCE

For the aspiring poet, the study of the ancients was not merely an academic task or intellectual discipline. Rather, this study provided him both the model and the inspiration for his own verse. Here was a place of poetic inheritance, and now was the time to try one's own song. The shepherd's world and the student's world share a startlingly similar end: "The poet comes to Arcadia for a clarification of his artistic, intellectual and moral purpose. The assumption of the shepherd's weeds signalizes for a millennium and more a commitment to poetry and to the exploration of the relative worths

of the active and contemplative existences. The temporary retire-
ment to the interior landscape becomes a preparation for engagement with the world of reality, for it is necessary for knowledge to
precede action" (Marinelli, 45). We need not substitute scholar's
gown for shepherd's weeds in the above description to see the connection between the literary and historical worlds. What Marinelli
says of Arcadia is essentially true of the Renaissance university. "It
is in Arcadia," he observes, that the shepherd/poet explores "his
commitment to the arts of poetry and to the art of love in its widest
sense" (46). It is in the university, I argue, that the student/poet explores these very same commitments, and thereby prepares for engagement with the greater world, specifically the very center of that
greater world: the court. If successful, the student of poetry
emerges from the university world, like the Arcadian poet, as the
inheritor of a great tradition of poetry. The difficulty he then faces
is how to live in the world without squandering his precious inheritance.

This engagement with the greater world requires first a departure
from the campus, a departure recorded—step by "stayed step"—in
the twelve months of Spenser's *Calender*. Moving beyond the walls
of Pembroke meant leaving behind fellowship, rivalry, poverty,
and, to an extent, even the common song; forgoing, as it were, "the
delights of youth generally." These pastoral joys did not vanish al-
together, but neither would they ever be quite the same. The shepherds of *Colin Cloutes Come Home Againe*, published some fifteen
years after the *Calender*, are middle-aged courtiers in thin bucolic
disguise. Among his many other objections to these shepherds,
"masked with faire dissembling curtesie" (1.700), Colin complains
that they lack collegiality and respect for learning:

> No art of schoole, but Courtiers schoolery
> For arts of schoole have there small countenance,
> Counted but toyes to busie ydle braines:
> And there professours find small maintenance,
> But to be instruments of other gaines.
>
> (701–6)

Gone are the scholar-poet-shepherds who peopled the *Calender*,
and gone for Spenser is the world that had furnished them forth, the
collegiate world of youth that had allowed for postponement of
real-world responsibilities and the neglect of *negotium* in favor of
otium.

Like the poet in Marinelli's description, Spenser had come to Cambridge for a clarification of his artistic, intellectual, and moral purpose. As the English inheritor of the classic pastoral tradition, Spenser spent his inheritance in a particular fashion, one that records not just the emergence of the poet from pastoral to heroic epic, but, even more precisely, the emergence of the poet from the campus to the court. To explore the latter world and ignore the former is to ignore this movement, and see but the political portion of the English pastoral, to see in effect the greater world to which the poet travels, and miss the world to which he bids adieu.

Phineas Fletcher did not so easily bid farewell to the world of his youth. He remained at Cambridge off and on for fifteen years. Finally, with his most productive years as a poet behind him, and exhausted by his long struggle for a permanent post at Cambridge, "the Spencer of his age"[17] exiled himself to Risley, where, employed as a chaplain, he took to pasturing a spiritual flock, writing devout religious meditations: *Joy in Tribulation* and *A Father's Testament*.

Milton, though he later criticized many of the methods of Cambridge in his *Prolusiones Oratoriae*, faced more difficulty than either Spenser or Fletcher in leaving the university and engaging in the greater world. Choosing not to stay on at Cambridge as a fellow, and declining the clerical profession, Milton apparently chose "to adopt no profession at all, but to live on as a mere student and a volunteer now and then in the service of the muses" (Masson, 333). Milton's later yields more than justified this initial loitering beneath the cumbersome burden of poetic inheritance. His reluctance, like that of his pastoral predecessors, was but the reluctance of youth faced with departure from itself.

3

Colin Clout's "Stayed Steps"

Precisely to where Colin Clout wanders after his wintry departure from the world of *The Shepheardes Calender* we are not told, but judging from his appearance atop Mount Acidale in Book VI of *The Faerie Queene*, he did not wander far. When, at the end of the December Eclogue, he bid adieu to the woods, his little lambs, his dear, his delights, and to good Hobbinol, he did so, if we take him at his word, "in his latter terme," as an old man awaiting death. However, when we range with Calidore through the fields abroad, we stumble upon a "jolly shepheard" producing "the merry sound / Of a shrill pipe" that holds, not only his own love and the three Graces, but a hundred other naked maidens "dancing in delight." Hardly the activity of old age. "Poore Colin Clout (who knowes not Colin Clout?)" (x.16.4).[1] He knows not Colin Clout, perhaps, who has read *The Shepheardes Calender* and seen him with a face in which "deepe furrowes old hath pight," his "head besprent with hoary frost," and the crow's-feet by his eye (134–36), and has watched him lay delight "abedde" and hang his pipe upon a tree. "Winter is come," the aged swain proclaimed at his departure, "And after winter commeth timely death" (149). The spectacle to which we, with Calidore, are treated on Mount Acidale, however, is hardly wintry, let alone close to death. Colin Clout, in fact, seems restored to eternal spring, complete with a new love, leaving the reader to wonder just how old is this aging swain?

Granted, our poet is not obliged to begin the latter pastoral episode where his early collection of eclogues leaves off, but neither can the responsible reader ignore the central presence of Colin Clout, which connects the earlier pastoral poem with the present epic canto. The rhetorical question signaling this connection—who, indeed, does not know Colin Clout?—is highlighted, rather than subverted, by the parenthesis. And when Colin reacts to Calidore's

62

intrusion by smashing his pipe, the connection between the two Colins is made comically explicit. To regard these two Colins as the
same character, however, requires that we account for his apparent
reversed aging. This problem is largely ignored by most readers of
the two poems, who allow the poet to not so "secretly shadoweth
himself" in Colin Clout for eleven eclogues only to see him throw
off his withered, pastoral husk in December and emerge as Immerito, England's new poet. Meanwhile, Colin Clout, "his body in-
scribed . . . with images of winter death,"[2] presumably hobbles
away, having served his inaugural, poet-making purpose. This traditional understanding of Colin's relation to Spenser, which I have
here caricatured, is nonproblematic until we come upon the rejuve-
nated, piping shepherd upon Mount Acidale and are confronted
with the poet's parenthetical rhetorical question. In consideration of
the imbedded complexity of that question, I offer an alternative to
the traditional understanding of the aged Colin Clout whom the
poet presents to us. Rather than conveniently separating Colin
Clout from Edmund Spenser when the former becomes too old for
writing heroic verse, I propose that we leave the poet shadowed in
his pastoral disguise and reconsider the matter of his apparent
aging. That this swain's youth has passed by December is quite
clear, but that he is, as he claims, an old man seems to me far less
certain. His "frostie season" is not, I think, to be taken too literally,
and the artist of the woodcut apparently did not think so either. Un-
less England's new poet is to walk forth leaning upon a cane, however, we must account for the furrowed skin, hoary frost, and
crow's-feet that Colin imagines himself to be wearing by the *Calender*'s end. My aim in this chapter is to examine more closely the
self-described posturing of Colin Clout as he both moves and stands
still in *The Shepheardes Calender*. The *Calender*, taken as a whole,
I argue, is a narrative in which Colin Clout comes of age, but not,
as he would have us believe, to old age.

Colin's youth, spent scaling craggy oaks to disrupt the raven's
nest and spilling nuts from the stately walnut tree—his "looser
yeares" of song and "musicks mirth"—we hear about, but never
see. By the time the poem commences in January, Colin's circumstance appropriately mimics two-headed Janus, after whom the
month is named. He is both forward- and backward-looking: forward because he stands as the initial figure in a twelve-month calendar of eclogues; backward because he imagines his "libertee and
lyfe" to be newly vanished and has turned suddenly—and pasto-

rally—retrospective. As Love's prisoner, chilled by Rosalind's coldness, he complains: "My life bloud [is] friesing vnkindly cold. . . . As if my years were wast, and woxen old" (1.26, 28). The "*As if*" with which Colin qualifies his description indicates that his sudden aging is of the Petrarchan kind, and suitably he speaks in Petrarchan extremes that leave out the middle seasons, the ripeness and maturity of middle age into which he is evolving. His "spring begonne," Colin thinks only of winter. No longer *adulescentia*, he can only fancy himself *senex*. The actual effects of the first-love wound are, of course, less dramatic. Experience replaces naivete, innocence gives way to unexpected pain, and responsibility threatens to replace the carelessness of one's early nest-wrecking years. Colin's reluctance to accept these changes is what keeps him both backward- and forward-looking and determines his despondent movement through the *Calender* toward his eventual departure from the world to which he is no longer suited.

Colin's initial reaction to Rosalind's scorn is to imitate it. As he plays the fool to her, he makes Hobbinol the fool to him. Colin, the finest maker of pastoral songs, not only calls his friend's love offerings clownish, but takes them and gives them to Rosalind, who scorns not just Colin singularly, but "rurral musick" and "Shepheards deuise" generally. Here in his imitation of Rosalind's scorn—a scorn that comes from outside the pastoral world—lies the key to Colin's rapid aging. The breaking of a pastoral friendship is one thing; the breaking of a pastoral pipe quite another. The former may be mended; the latter is a gift of Pan and the Muses whom Colin—the pastoral piper turned Petrarchan complainer—scolds for their failure to comfort him:

> Yet for thou [Pan] pleaseth not, where most I would:
> And thou vnlucky Muse, that wonst to ease
> My musing mynd, yet canst not, when though should
> Both pype and Muse, shall some the while abye
> So broke his oaten pype, and downe dyd lye.

> (1.68–72)

The broken pipe, like the broken friendship with Hobbinol, is but the measure of Colin's broken heart, and while it may not make him suddenly aged, it gives him immediate cause to describe himself so. For old age was a well-known Renaissance excuse for the failure to create "song."

In his article "When Did a Man in the Renaissance Grow Old?" Creighton Gilbert presents evidence that age, along with love, was offered as an excuse for lack of productivity.[3] When, for example, Pieto Aretino, at age forty-five, finds that the rate of his literary composition has diminished, he complains: "Old age is slowing down my wits, and love, which ought to stimulate them, is putting them to sleep; I used to do forty stanzas in a morning, now I barely assemble one." Colin Clout, his broken pipe on the ground, suffers from a similar problem of productivity, and offers the same twofold excuse of age and love to explain why he "forbeare[s] / His wonted songs, wherein he all outwent" (April, 15–16). Men in the Renaissance, Gilbert says, often exaggerated their age, and commonly described themselves as "old" in their mid-forties or even their late thirties. Erasmus, Gilbert notes, composed his poem "On the Discomforts of Old Age" when he was still thirty-nine years old. Colin's complaints of hoary frost merely echo the habits of the Renaissance, and though he fancies himself to be an aged swain, he is more likely seeing his first grey hairs than his last.

His pipe, heart, and friendship all broken, Colin waits until the following winter, one full year later, before finally bidding adieu to each of these delights and departing from the pastoral world. Determined to depart, he loiters for the length of a twelve-month calendar. The emblems or mots[4] that the poet assigns to Colin during this time do little to illustrate his relationship to the pastoral world in which he remains even while having forsaken its joys. The January and June emblems offer instead Petrarchan descriptions that reflect the particular circumstance of Colin's love enterprise with Rosalind, for which in January there is still hope, however faint, *Anchora Speme*. By June, Colin's hope that Rosalind might yet return his love is utterly extinguished: *Gia speme spente*. Neither the faint nor the extinguished hope that these emblems describe helps us to understand Colin's movement and lack of movement through the eclogues that bring us at long last to his departure from the pastoral in December. The religious motto that serves as Colin's emblem in the November Eclogue, *La mort ny mord*, while it offers anonymous hope, illustrates neither Colin's Petrarchan ruin nor his pastoral posture.

That the assigned emblems do little to illustrate Colin's posture within the pastoral world from which he promises to depart should not surprise readers of the poem. Rosemary Freeman was perhaps the first to point out that "apart from the use of mottoes, *The Sheph-*

eardes Calender is not particularly emblematic" (102). John
Bender adds to Freeman's observation that poetry of debate and
"the *copia* of pictorial imagery" are essentially incompatible.[5]
Such observations, while they characterize the *Calender*'s scarcity
of pictorial image, may also underestimate and even conceal pictorial imagery where it does exist in the *Calender*, not just in the fa-
bles or the traditional elevation of Queen Elizabeth in the April
Eclogue, but in the movement of the *Calender*'s central figure
through the poem. Insofar as *The Shepheardes Calender* is poetry
of debate, it affords little pictorial imagery. However, insofar as the
poem comprises a pastoral narrative—the story of Colin Clout's departure from the pastoral world at which he had formerly been the
center—proper understanding of that narrative relies upon the ekphrastic descriptions that Colin offers of himself. Observing that
"purely poetic emblem productions" of the sixteenth century "de-
rived from the ancient tradition of ekphrastic poetry," Bender notes
that readers of Elizabethan poetry may be "passing over many figures which may once have called emblems to the mind's eye" (84).

Not twenty lines into the opening eclogue of the *Calender*, Colin
Clout cuts just such an emblematic figure. A cold and dissatisfied
Narcissus, he sees himself reflected in the frozen world around him,
or, more immediately, the frozen earth beneath him: "Thou barrein
ground, whome winters wrath hath wasted / Art made a myrrhour,
to behold my plight" (19–20). What to do when the character in
whom the poet has shadowed himself sees himself reflected in the
world that the poet has created? Lest the poignancy of this reflective
moment be somehow lost upon the reader, Colin's exclamation
contains a rather explosive verbal trope. His pun, "Art made a
myrrhour" is not only fulfilled in its very construction, but in the
Calender as a whole, which serves as an exercise in artistic self-
portraiture.[6] The poet's art, his poem, serves, in effect, as a mirror
in which he and his readers see his reflected self.

In the June Eclogue, we find Colin, smashed pipe at his feet, explaining to his companion Hobbinol why he can no longer enjoy
the place of "pierlesse pleasures" in which Hobbinol invites him to
stay. His reason, not surprisingly, has much to do with his increased
age. No longer consumed by the great heat of his Petrarchan impulse, Colin now plays the knowledgeable elder, immune to such
youthful folly. The condescending tone of this swain, now in his
"ryper age," suggests that the friendship between the two swains is
not quite mended, and one wonders why this distraught shepherd—

in, but not of, this place—has remained through the spring to see the coming of summer, another season with which he is entirely out of synchrony.

By way of explanation, Colin invites the reader to see him in his own art just as he had previously seen himself reflected in nature's. Discarding the "rhymes and roundelayes" that, Hobbinol reminds him, he was "wont on wastfull hylls to singe," Colin speaks instead of the pragmatic, pictorial function of his present verse:

> I wote my rymes bene rough, and rudely drest
> The fytter they my careful case to frame.
> Enough is me to paint out my unrest.
>
> (77–79)

Colin's talk of framing and painting here is no more incidental than his reassertion of art's mirroring qualities. Earlier in this same eclogue, he has already made good on his "rudely drest" words by painting his unrest and framing his careful case:

> I whylst youth, and course of carelesse yeeres
> Did let me walke withouten lincks of loue,
> In such delights did joy amongst me peeres:
> But ryper age such pleasures doth reproue,
> My fancye eke from former follies moue
> To stayed steps: for time in passing weares
> (As garments doen, which wexen old aboue)
> And draweth newe delightes with hoary heares.
>
> (33–40)

Besides the predictable "hoary heares" on his head, Colin offers us here a particular ekphrastic detail that describes his precise circumstance.

His fancy has moved, he says, "from former follies. . . . To stayed steps." Colin stands, or rather steps, upon feet that are *stayed*. The word, even in Spenser's day, suggested several possible meanings, which, at the very least, can be sectioned into two denotations: supported and encumbered.[7] This is the very circumstance of Colin Clout. He stands firm, but not, as it were, upon solid ground. Rather, he remains on pastoral soil, unable on "stayed steps" to move forward, to depart. Consider a definition (current by 1533) of *stay*: "to scruple, be in doubt, raise difficulties," as well as the more

familiar definition of the same word (current by 1591): "Delay . . .
to withhold for a time; to postpone."[8]

Stayed steps, in fact, describe both the movement and lack of
movement in Colin's prolonged departure. Where does one go upon
steps that withhold one for a time? Such steps are but the shuffling
feet of a man at a crossroads, a crossroads of, say, ambition and
reminiscence. In Colin's self-described posture, of which the January woodcut offers an ekphrastic illustration, we recognize the classical "contrapposta hallowed by Greco-Roman statuary." Colin
Clout, one foot firmly planted, steps forward with the other. He has
a walking staff, but it rests against his leaning shoulders. He is "neither walking nor standing still."[9] Howard Hibbard describes the
posture as an "asymmetrical arrangement of limbs, with the weight
borne chiefly by one leg, which gives a sense of the normal action
of gravity and the possibility of movement" (56). Interestingly,
Hibbard describes this posture in Michelangelo's David, where he
sees the young artist offering "a heroically idealized version of
himself" in a "psychologically charged pause of apprehension," a
moment, not of triumph, but "troubled ambition" (61).[10] Whether
or not we accept Hibbard's close-up analysis of David—and indeed, of Michelangelo in David—his observations can be applied
to the more deliberately self-conscious work of Edmund Spenser,
who, shadowed in the contrapose of a far less famous shepherd,
stands in pastoral anonymity and steps toward epic fame.

This counterbalanced posture of Colin Clout's is itself emblematic, suggestive of the popular Renaissance prescription for maturity: *festina lente*, or make haste slowly. The popularity of
Augustus's maxim during the Renaissance is indicated by the numerous and varied emblems that accompanied it. Edgar Wind men-
tions, besides the familiar dolphin wrapped about an anchor (partly
alluded to by the anchora in Colin's mots), a tortoise with a sail on
its back, a diamond ring entwined with foliage, and a butterfly atop
a crab. In 1557 one finds the motto illustrated by a dolphin wrapped
around a chameleon,[11] and by 1565 the settled anchor and swift dolphin have somehow evolved into a slow snake encircling a swift
arrow.[12]

Beyond the emblem books, in works of art slow hastening is seen
most clearly in the contrapposta of young figures caught in the frozen movement of maturity. Making the connection between the
posture and the maxim in a sixteenth-century fresco, Wind offers a

description that recalls both the circumstance and posture of Colin Clout:

> In a fresco designed in the style of Mantegna, a swift, winged-footed figure of Chance, her eyes covered by her forelock, incites a youth to grasp her quickly as she passes before him on a rolling sphere. Behind the youth a steady, quiet figure of Wisdom restrains his eager steps. . . . The youth, while placed under the protection of restraining Virtue . . . is quite intent in his pursuit of outward Chance. . . . His action, at once eager and steady, is a perfect embodiment of *festina lente*: he hastens slowly. (102–3)

So too Colin Clout, who enjoys the protection of the pastoral world yet, in the frantic ire of a broken heart and pipe, attempts to make haste from that world. If not eager and steady, he is, in the course of the twelve months, determined and despondent—determined to leave youth behind, yet not until twelve months later finally departing slowly, held back by nostalgic reminiscence. He goes forward, looking backward.

I offer just one more example to illustrate what I believe to be the emblematic significance of Colin Clout's stayed steps. In their simultaneous motion and stillness, the three Graces of Botticelli's *Primivera* are *festina lente* danced. "In so far as dialectic can be danced," Wind says, "it has been accomplished in this group. 'Opposition', 'concord', and 'concord in opposition', all three are expressed in the postures and steps and the articulate style of joining hands" (118–19).[13] Colin's posture and circumstance in the *Calender* bear a particular resemblance to the middle of the three Graces. Castitas (Chastity), like Colin, is a neophyte victim of Cupid's arrow. The hovering, blindfolded god in Botticelli's painting directs his flaming weaponry precisely at the heart of Castitas, who is being "initiated into Love by the ministrations of Voluptas [Fruitfulness] and Pulchritudo [Beauty]" (Wind, 119). It is Castitas's dance of initiation that the Graces dance. Urged forward by Beauty, who still grasps her hand, the stationary figure of Chastity, with her front foot firmly planted, steps with her back foot toward the inviting figure of Fruitfulness. With her left shoulder unveiled, Castitas appears to be moving toward Voluptas unrestrained; however, Voluptas presents counter movements toward Castitas, which, ironically, restrain Castitas—slow, as it were, her hastening forward. In *The Shepheardes Calender*, I believe, the poet has similarly choreographed the initiation of "the neophyte," Colin Clout. Having felt his initial love wound, Colin is urged forward by the beauty of Rosalind toward eventual maturity. The January woodcut shows him staring, like Castitas, toward that which he hopes will be. He steps with his front foot toward the world of passion (the town in which Rosalind presumably resides), even while he keeps his other foot firmly planted in the pastoral.

So too, I would argue, does this figure, partially planted in pastoral soil, reflect the very circumstance of the poet whom Colin "shadoweth." In Colin, I believe, we see the ruminative maturation, the "stayed steps," of Edmund Spenser himself. Testing his poetic talents in the initiative genre of pastoral, Spenser looks toward the more ambitious, more "fruitful," and more urbane endeavor of epic poetry, an endeavor that will require, among other things, stepping from the private praise of a Rosalind to the public praise of a fairy queen. Such a transference, I think, inspires reluctance for artistic as well as political reasons. One gets some sense of the poet's pastoral apprehension if one imagines *The Faerie Queene*—as Spenser himself was forced to—as yet unwritten. The smashing of the pastoral pipe may be done in *haste*, but the subsequent turning to "those, that weld the awful crowne"[14] is something one does, understandably, *slowly*.

Recognition of this slow hastening as the governing circumstance of the poem's overall movement places one at a critical crossroads of sorts between those who read the poem as Colin's clear rejection of the pastoral in favor of the heroic, and those who read it as Colin's mournful loss of paradise. Both arguments are familiar. A. C. Hamilton, for example, regards "the argument of *The Shepheardes Calender* [as] the rejection of the pastoral life for the truly dedicated life in the world. For Spenser, this is to serve the Queen by inspiring her people to all virtuous action" ("Argument," 176). Harry Berger, on the other hand, using the "paradise principle," numbers Colin among those who have lost paradise through thwarted love ("Aging Boy," 27). Colin, in the first case, is perceived as active, having rejected pastoral, and in the second as passive, having lost the pastoral. To adopt too strictly either of these readings is to have to choose between *festina* or *lente*. Spenser himself likely faced such a choice in the emblem books available to him.

We find, for example, the image of a familiar youth in *Minerva Britanna*, printed by Henry Peacham:[15] His right hand holds a bel-

lows to his ear / His left, the quick, and speedy spur doth bear."
This emblematic representation of *Capriccio*[16] (Capriciousness), recalls Colin's hasty smashing of his own bagpipe in January. The
verse that accompanies Peacham's figure, however, illustrates the
contrast between this youth and the halting rashness of Colin Clout:

> Such is Capriccio, or th'*unstayed* mind,
> Whome thousand times hourly do possess,
> For riding post, with every blast of wind,
> In nought he's steady, save unstableness.

Just such instability is, in fact, what is promised in the epistle preceding *The Shepheardes Calender*: "Onely this appeareth, that his
unstayed yougth had long wandred in the common Labyrinth of
Love." Colin's capricious pipe-smashing in the first eclogue shows
us such an unstayed youth. His subsequent wandering from youth
toward maturity, from pastoral toward heroic, is measured, quite literally, in twelve months. During this time the shepherd-poet attempts to become what his feet describe, *staid*, that is: "settled in
character; of grave or sedate deportment; dignified and serious of
demeanour or conduct; free from flightiness or *caprice* [emphasis
mine]. Of the intellect and intellectual operations: sober, steady,
well-regulated" (adjectival use of the past participle stayed,
O.E.D., 1557). This is the proper disposition for writing epic
poetry, which, after all, requires different "feet" than pastoral
verse. Thus, like Ovid before him, Spenser describes his reluctant
movement from one kind of poetry to the next by drawing attention
to the literal feet upon which he steps.[17]

By the *Calender*'s end, the "aged" Colin has forsworn his love
for Rosalind in order to sing of Eliza; he has bid adieu to the private
delights of the pastoral in order to engage in the public enterprise
of romantic epic. The crossroads at which he lingers after the initial
smashing of his pastoral pipe twelve months earlier is, I argue, the
same at which Spenser himself stood in his departure from the
groomed gardens of Pembroke College, replete with the youthful
delights of the academic world, for the more precarious and more
public world of the Elizabethan court. Spenser was not creating in
Colin Clout a stationary caricature of himself, but he was, I believe,
recording his own poetic maturity,[18] which, while it took him beyond pastoral, also brought him first to pastoral, and would return
him there again in *The Faerie Queene*.

This time, after nearly six full books of epic romance, we come upon what I believe is the climactic vision of the entire *Faerie Queene*. Calidore has left behind the public world of heroic quest and entered a world of pastoral romance. He has not simply laid his armor idly by for an afternoon, but put on shepherd's weeds indefinitely, and we, with the poet's permission ("Ne certes mote he greatly blamed be"), gladly loiter with him. By the time he ranges across the fields to Mount Acidale, Calidore is at six removes from the slanderous public world of the court from which he began his chase.[19] Thus far from the court of Gloriana, "far from all peoples troad," whom should he find but Colin Clout, bagpipe very much intact, piping a vision that stops Calidore in his curious tracks.

We remain, with this pseudo-shepherd, "in the covert wood," gazing upon the extravagant private vision of a hundred naked maidens encircling three, encircling one "whose sundry parts were here too long to tell / But she that in the midst of them did stand / Seem'd all the rest in beauty to excell" (x.14.2–4). She whom all the other Graces graced is not Venus, nor Eliza, but Colin's own private beloved.[20] Thus we return near the end of *The Faerie Queene* not just to the pastoral, but to that from which the pastoral springs, the personal. Colin mediates not his own dance of initiation, but a lavish dance of maturity—both personal and poetic. The ripeness disguised as old age at the *Calender*'s end is here fulfilled. There are neither crow's-feet, white hairs, nor any tropological need for them, for the romantic epic only hoped for by the stayed swain of the *Calender* now nears its completion. The pastoral, which he had abandoned in order to sing this public song, now affords him some small personal rest that he takes, nonetheless, with an elaborate apology to the one to whom his private digression is most likely to give offense:

> Great Gloriana, greatest Majesty,
> Pardon thy shepheard, mongst so many layes,
> As he hath sung of thee in all his dayes,
> To make one minime of thy poore handmayd,
> And underneath thy feete to place her prayse,
> That when thy glory shall be farre displayed
> To future age of her this mention may be made.
>
> (x.28.3–9)

Colin's pastoral vision, which is every bit a private affair, is cut short by the public intrusion of Calidore, a clumsy discourtesy in which the reader unwittingly participates. This time, after "breaking his bagpipe quight," Colin stays a "long time" with Calidore upon Mount Acidale, whose pastoral delights surpass the ones for which he told Hobbinol he was too old. The two men linger until Calidore, not Colin, hastens "as the wounded Whale" back to his beloved. As Colin had been, so is Calidore now suffering the initiation of that "enuenimd sting." The reader departs the pastoral with Calidore, leaving Colin Clout in comfortable pastoral residence. Colin, it seems, had been mistaken in his prolonged but hastened departure from the world of the *Calender*. His "adieu delights" might more accurately have been delivered as "au revoir, delights." "After winter commeth" not timely death, but spring. After first love, second love. And, as E. K.'s interpretation of the absent December emblem[21] suggests, after poetic debut cometh poetic maturity. Colin's mistaken adieu can be credited in part to the artistic anxiety of Edmund Spenser, who, if unable to produce the epic for which *The Shepheardes Calender* had been a preparation, had, in the grey-headed Colin Clout, produced, just in case, the Renaissance's hoary-frosted excuse.

4

"Shepheardes Delights"

"OF ALL THE CAMBRIDGE SINGERS," ARTHUR GRAY WRITES IN HIS
history of Cambridge, "Edmund Spenser may be said to reflect
most characteristically the influences of his university education.
. . . To his student time at Cambridge Spenser largely owed his Puri-
tanism, the Platonic and Aristotelean colouring of his poetry, and
. . . the influences of the critical coterie to which he belonged"
(143–44). Such a debt—and I do not think Gray's claim exaggerated—is itself reason for fond remembrance. In chapter 2, I described what other remembrances I thought Spenser and others
might have held of their time at Cambridge. Having examined in
the previous chapter what I believe to be the essentially youthful
nature of Colin Clout and the world of the *Calender* from which he
departs, I turn my attention here to the particular pastoral ingredients of the *Calender* in which we see the poem's reminiscent connection to the world of the university from which Spenser had
recently departed.

Coming to the poem with this point of view, I wish my reading
to be a suggestive rather than a prescriptive one. *The Shepheardes
Calender*, taken as a whole in all its complexity, does not present a
single coherent argument about life, university or otherwise. Referring to attempts that would find one single meaning in the *Calender*, Isabel MacCaffrey wisely points out that such readings
"underestimate the power of the poet's imagination, its world-
making energy, its drive toward comprehensiveness, its urge to include rather than exclude meanings." Such descriptions, she says,
"ignore certain of its [the poem's] elements which may not con-
form to the proposed pattern" (89). Ironically, the elements that
have been most ignored in the insistence upon a proposed structure,
and more recently, upon a proposed politic, are the fundamental ingredients of pastoral poetry—the delights that Colin Clout must

74

leave behind. Where "world-making energy" is concerned, these "delights of youth generally," as the gloss calls them, are well worth our attention. For though the world that Spenser makes is permanent, youthful delights are not.

If the only authentic delight to be found in the *Calender* is the birth of a heroic poet, for which we wait the whole of twelve eclogues, we ought to be greatly disappointed by the weary, hoary-haired figure who emerges at the *Calender*'s end. If, on the other hand, we take seriously, not just the epic task to which Colin aspires, but the pastoral world to which he bids farewell, then the "delights" he catalogues in his departure can be more closely considered. Are the general joys of youth merely the shallow occupations of what Piers calls "a world's childe"? Where in the *Calender* is there delight enough to heal a broken heart? What, after all, replaces Colin's singing but shepherds' bickering and ecclesiastical complaining? The joys explicated in chapter 2 may well be part of a recollected collegiate world, but where do we find them in *The Shepheardes Calender*?

We find these pastoral joys of youth, fellowship, poverty, and rivalry, I believe, in essentially two places, the first being in what I have called "the backward look," the nostalgic perspective by which the pastoral joys of youth are usually presented. This nostalgic perspective, as I argued in the last chapter, belonged to Spenser himself, who, having left behind the world of Pembroke, consequently created several shepherds who eloquently enumerate the youthful delights that they once knew and now have lost. The chief among them is Colin himself, who, in the June Eclogue, recalls his carefree years before his love attachment:

> And I whylst youth, and course of carelesse yeeres
> Did let me walke withouten lincks of loue,
> In such delights did joy amongst my peeres:
> But ryper age such pleaures doth reproue.
>
> (1.33–36)

"Ryper" age reproves such pleasures, but it also rues their absence. In fact, as Berger points out, it often reproves them because it misses them ("Aging Boy," 29). As Patrick Cullen divides pastoral shepherds into Mantuan (bound by rational duty),[1] and Arcadian (set loose by nature), Berger divides them similarly into those who have found paradise and those who have lost it. He finds that "both

love of youthful pleasures and bitterness at their loss are sedi-
mented into the [pastoral] tradition, which is handed down from
one generation to the next in a cyclic pattern dominated by the paradise principle" ("Aging Boy," 27). Those who have lost paradise,
Berger notes, have lost it through thwarted love (e.g., Colin Clout),
or through experience of the actual world and its evils (Thenot,
Piers). As we will see in the case of Thenot, the speeches delivered
by those who have lost paradise are typically angry denouncements
of the frivolous and transitory nature of the delights by which the
young shepherds are distracted. Even beneath this bitterness, however, lies a nostalgic longing for those very delights. This longing
is generally not very well concealed beneath the postured speeches,
which contain fond, detailed descriptions of the same joys they condemn.

Nor are those shepherds who have found paradise freed from a
nostalgic longing for that which is lost. They may be enjoying
youthful delights, but their paradise is incomplete without the chief
delights of song and fellowship. In *The Shepheardes Calender* both
the singing of Colin Clout and the fellowship the shepherds enjoyed
with him are taken away when his love for Rosalind goes unrequited. Rosalind's unfaithfulness not only wounds Colin but frac-
tures as well the pastoral circle of which he was a part. Thus it is
that Colin is spoken of fondly and sorrowfully by Hobbinol and
others:

> But for the ladde, whome long I lovd so deare,
> Nowe loues a lasse, that all his loue doth scorne:
> He plongd in payne, his tressed locks dooth teare.
> Shepheards delights he dooth them all forsweare,
> His pleasaunt Pipe, whych made vs meriment,
> He wylfully hath broke, and doth forbeare
> His wonted songs, wherein he all outwent.
>
> (April, l.11–16)

Hobbinol here laments the loss of the two joys most central to "the
paradise" he has found. His first loss is the affection of Colin,
which is now given instead to one who scorns it. Hobbinol's second
loss is the loss of Colin's songs, which have been replaced by silence and hair-tearing grief.

"The way out of the labyrinth of man's grief is not through pastoral song," says Hamilton. "The failure of pastoral song," he claims,

"suggests Spenser's impatience with pastoral genre" ("Grene Path," 13). I find neither the failure of pastoral song nor Spenser's impatience with the genre borne out in the poem. Even the explicit impatience of Colin in the first eclogue gives way to eleven more months of contemplation of what lies ahead and behind. Only after smashing his pipe and cursing Pan and the muses does Colin Clout begin to see that pastoral song cannot fail at what it does not promise to do. It does not propose to lead man out of the labyrinth of his grief; nor will epic poetry accomplish this. Such a labyrinth is necessarily a private one, whose passages cannot be revealed by any general map—pastoral, epic, or otherwise. Colin has been wronged in love by Rosalind; his consequent failure to be consoled by song is his own struggle. MacCaffrey recognizes this when she finds that Hobbinol fails to "cure" Colin: "Poetry [pastoral or epic] cannot provide a talisman against death, nor heal the wounds of love, nor recreate the state of innocence" (105). Removing pain is not the place of pastoral poetry. Its job is to comfort and reconcile humankind to that pain. As Paul Alpers puts it: "The great pastoral poets are directly concerned with the extent to which song that gives present pleasure can comfort, and if not transform and celebrate, then accept and reconcile man to the stresses and realities of his situation" ("Eclogue Tradition," 353). What pastoral poetry can do is what Spenser's *Calender* does—provide an ekphrastic hold upon that which has been lost.

This paradoxical quality of pastoral song—its ability to preserve but not recover what is lost—exemplifies the dual nature of all of the pastoral joys. At times pastoral song serves only to provide present pleasure, and as such it may be considered by Thenot and Piers as one of the frivolous delights of unwise youth. At other times, however, pastoral song attempts to reconcile human loss and transform that loss into something permanent. It does not guarantee such a transformation, but it does offer the possibility. In this sense, pastoral song is not only an authentic delight, but a profound one, deserving the fond "adieu" Colin bids it.

Like song, fellowship aims at more than present pleasure. The paradise of the *locus amoenus* remains available to Hobbinol because he knows no Rosalind. The *locus amoenus*, in other words, has more to do with emotions than landscape. Hobbinol, unlike Colin, enjoys a sort of state of grace wrought by circumstance. Untroubled by a Rosalind, he avails himself instead of the fellowship, of his shepherd companions. His love, if unanswered by Colin, remains constant nonetheless, and when he sings, he sings the songs of Colin. That paradise remains even a remote possibility for Colin depends upon fellowship, which sustains the world of the poem, not only in the face of Colin's severe melancholy and eventual departure, but in the face of storms of injustice and even death. Colin cracks his pipe when there are still eleven eclogues to go. His sorrow and broken pipe can sustain nothing but a lengthy, and somewhat redundant, elegy. No wonder then that Hamilton finds that the *Calender* traces only the tragic vision of life. Yet the poem is not an elegy, nor is its vision purely tragic. Death, on more than one level, plays its part certainly, and Colin's movement from deep sorrow to determined departure calls upon elegiac elements; yet, more prominent throughout the poem is the fellowship among the shepherds with which each eclogue is wrought.

As Hamilton himself notes, "each eclogue centers upon the pastoral metaphor of care," and "the three concluding eclogues are climactic as they treat the proper care of the shepherd-poet" ("Grene Path," 16). The poem's dependence upon the fundamental joy of fellowship is demonstrated in the fact that only in the first and the last of the twelve eclogues does a shepherd appear alone. In both cases, the lone shepherd is Colin Clout, whose chief loss is ultimately not romantic, but pastoral.

Present fellowship, then, is the second place where we find the pastoral joys residing in *The Shepheardes Calender*. "There is not," Hallett Smith notes, "a core something wrapped up in a covering of pastoral . . . the pastoral idea, in its various ramifications, is the *Calender*" (46). That "pastoral idea" Smith agrees to call *otium*, the various ramifications of which we have become acquainted with in the previous chapters. *Otium*, we recall, is the ultimate result of the pastoral fellowship that sustains the shepherds' world when grief and hardship would otherwise erode it.

The pastoral joy of rivalry is built into *The Shepheardes Calender*, with its Mantuanesque and Arcadian shepherds in direct opposition to one another. Were this dichotomy only a symbolic one, for the sake of rhetorical or moral debate, there would be no actual rivalry, no delight in the conversations between the shepherds. As it is, however, the shepherds are characters, not types, or, as Cullen puts it, "the debates are debates between personalities as well as perspectives" (33). Because of this, their exchanges contain the elements of sport, frolic, and defiance described in chapter 2. Just as the delights of song and fellowship have been often overlooked by critics who focus on the poem's structural movement and neglect its human ingredients, so too with the joy of rivalry. This oversight, as Cullen points out, has resulted in part from a "failure to recognize the human comedy involved especially in the [poem's] framework." The comedy, Cullen notes, "ranges from the verbal fisticuffs characteristic of the singing-contest and the pastoral debate to a more sophisticated comedy of character" (33).

One way to recognize the inherent comedy that Cullen describes is to trace the word "delight" through the *Calender*. What emerges when we do so are two opposing worldviews[2] in dialogue with one another throughout the poem: "the Mantuanesque shepherds, whose contentious orthodoxy requires either that man revise the world radically or that he withdraw from it [and] Spenser's Arcadian shepherds [who] want to share in whatever fun and joy that the world may have to offer" (Cullen, 31).

The Arcadian shepherd has, in Berger's words, "found paradise." As a speaker he is "recreative" because, being in paradise, he sees no reason for leaving it ("Aging Boy," 27). Here we find Cuddie, Willye, Pierce, Hobbinol, and Palinode (if he only could). Opposite these "careless" and contented swains stand Thenot and Piers along with Morrel and Diggon Davie, the "plaintive" or Mantuan shepherds to whom paradise has been lost.[3]

These discontented swains have, as noted earlier, lost paradise through "thwarted love" or through exposure to the evils of the actual world. Theirs is a private loss, though their explanations are inevitably general; they refer not to their own loss of paradise, but to Adam's loss, which is all of ours, as Morrel describes it in the July Eclogue:

> Till by his foly one did fall,
>   that all the rest did spill.
> And sithens shepheardes been foresayd
>   from places of delight.

(1.67–70)

That delight is no longer available to any shepherd is the sum of the Mantuanesque argument. "Ne in good or goodnes taken delight: / But kindle coales of conteck and yre" (1.85–86), says Diggon Davie in the September Eclogue.

While these shepherds are busy warning their companions that paradise is no longer available, the Arcadian shepherds alert their fellow swains that paradise is all about them, and invite them to enjoy its delights. Willye tells Thomalin in the March Eclogue: "Tho shall we sporten in delight, / And learne with Lettice to wexe light" (1.19–20). In the May Eclogue, Palinode attributes Piers's plaintive admonitions, not to Adam's loss but to Piers's own loss: "Sicker now I see thou speakest of spight / All for thou lackest somedele their [the young swains'] delight" (1.55–56).

The chief spokesman for the Arcadian shepherds is Colin's closest companion Hobbinol, and his invitation to Colin in the June Eclogue, as we saw in chapter 2, is the most fervent of all the shepherds. "Tell me, what wants me here to worke delyte?" he asks Colin, "I more delight then larke in sommer dayes" (3.51). Here in his world the "systers nyne / Doe make them musick, for their more delight" (1.29). Hobbinol is the character of the *locus amoenus*, that place of seeming timelessness which, though lost by Colin, is still available to him. What Piers says of Palinode applies to Hobbinol. He is, with Palinode, Willye, and Cuddie, "a worldes childe," a *pastoral* world's child.

Between Hobbinol and Piers stands Colin, who, while not in paradise, cannot, until the poem's completion, be counted among those who have lost it. And even then, as I have argued, his loss is not actually permanent. Since the *Calender* traces his reluctant movement toward this loss, and he is the one in whom Spenser figures himself, we return inevitably to the question of a central meaning to the poem. Hamilton's argument that the poem traces Spenser's rejection of pastoral in favor of heroic poetry is backed by his ill opinion of the pastoral poet, who he says "is self-regarding, being both in this world, and of it: he is as Piers says of Palinode 'a worldes childe' " ("Grene Path," 18).[4] Cuddie, who prefers to "feede youthes fancie," represents to Hamilton just such a world's child: "Cuddie finds inspiration in wine which only serves him for a while until his courage cools and he returns to the humble shade of the pastoral, presumably to nurse a hangover. For all his powers he is the failed poet who has no role in society and therefore no identity" ("Grene Path," 17). In this indictment of Cuddie, Hamilton echoes Piers, and recalls to us as well the Cambridge officials of chapter 2 who complained of youth's fancy.

Cuddie is indeed a world's child, but we must not disregard the article "a" in Piers's accusation of Palinode. Hamilton's statement that the pastoral poet is "of this world" is questionable. What the pastoral poet's relationship is to *this* world is not certain, but one thing is sure: Hobbinol and Colin are of a world quite apart from this world. They belong to a world, in fact, whose troubles come from *this* world. Theirs is a world of youthful delights, a world from which Colin must depart.

In his prolonged departure, Colin may well look forward to the task of epic verse, but this very ambition, as I argued in the previous chapter, is what keeps him frozen upon stayed steps. And, like the Colin in whom he has fashioned himself, Edmund Spenser cannot go forward to the future until he has first preserved the past, and it is for this that he has deliberately and successfully employed pastoral. Like Virgil before him, Spenser chose the youthful genre of pastoral to both test and fashion himself. "He ceased to be Master Edmund Spenser of Merchant Taylors' School and Pembroke College, Cambridge," Helgerson says, "and became Immerito, Colin Clout, the New Poet" (896). Eventually this would be true, but such a transformation, being neither easy nor sudden, is properly facilitated by the genre of pastoral. To fashion himself overtly as a student would be adverse to his aim of becoming a professional poet. To fashion himself as a court poet would be presumptuous and impossible. Thus Spenser's *Calender* is a record of his becoming, in which he fashions himself as fashioning himself.

Spenser's departure from Cambridge meant departure from his closest companion, Gabriel Harvey. Harvey, we learn from E. K., is shadowed in the poem under the guise of Hobbinol,[5] to whom Colin bids adieu at the poem's end. Their friendship and eventual parting is central to the poem's meaning. Richard Mallette's claim that "the most important aspect of the poet's life that the *Calender* examines is his love life," is true only insofar as the term "love life" is applied nonrestrictively to include Hobbinol as the original recipient of Colin's affections. As for Colin's romantic venture with Rosalind, we learn little apart from the standard Petrarchan predicament: he's so hot for her; she's so cold. We know that Rosalind's lack of interest is the chief cause of his sorrow, but we meet her only in the gossip of the other shepherds, and we never do hear the full story of her love affair with Colin. Colin's loss of Rosalind is a crucial aspect of a poem whose chief preoccupation is with loss; however, her scorn of Colin and his lowly trade is something we hear about only from Colin, and which, therefore, serves only as background to the poem. Hobbinol, on the other hand, is present to Colin throughout the eclogues. He appears in five of the eclogues and plays a major role in three of them. It is his friendship with

Colin, not Colin's failed love affair with Rosalind, that is the most important aspect of the poet's life examined by the *Calender*. The poem records the faithful love of Hobbinol for Colin. Colin's connectedness to Hobbinol reinforces and is at the center of his connectedness to the pastoral world. The poem is about Colin's disconnecting himself from that world and from the love of Hobbinol. The other eclogues, with their depictions of fellowship, consolation, and shepherd-to-shepherd dialogue, mirror the relationship of Hobbinol and Colin.

One need not agree with G. C. Moore Smith, in his introduction to Gabriel Harvey's *Marginalia*, that the *Calender* is "an eternal monument to the friendship of Edmund Spenser and Gabriel Harvey" (iii) in order to see the relationship of the two men pastoralized in a complex fashion in this poem. Nor is it necessary to trace with Paul McLane the similarity and dissimilarity of Hobbinol to Harvey. Hobbinol is not, as McLane says, a "dramatic presentation" of Harvey. Hobbinol is a poetic creation of Spenser's, the product of a poetic reimagining that may have sought to portray what he saw as the most splendid qualities of his friend's character. That the dreamy Hobbinol of *The Shepheardes Calender* is radically divergent from the sardonic realist whom we find in Harvey's *Letter-Book* ought to surprise us no more than that the Cambridge University Harvey inhabited was not much like "the paradise" Spenser has Hobbinol describe.

That Harvey and Hobbinol both appear to object to romantic love, for example, is quite true. However, the reasons why Harvey counts romantic love as ridiculous are different from those of Hobbinol. Harvey found romantic love to be ridiculous on several accounts: it caused inevitable misery; it was unrealistic; it knew no moderation, and it interfered with the fame that might be earned through public service (McLane, 255). Hobbinol's main objection to Colin's adventure in love is that it has jeopardized the preexisting love between himself and Colin ("the ladde, whome long I lovd so deare, / Nowe loues a lasse"). Romantic love has not only threatened his particular friendship with Colin, but it has removed Colin from the circle of fellowship and song and the *otium* he once knew. That Harvey had objections akin to these is not only possible but, as we have seen, quite likely. From what we know of him, however, such objections were not likely to show up in writing. Rather they are given voice in the world's child, Hobbinol, Spenser's poetic version of his Cambridge companion. That genuine and open disagreement existed between Spenser and Harvey indicates that their friendship, like the friendship between Colin and Hobbinol, was founded upon things more enduring, and apparently more fundamental, than either temperament or philosophies. Theirs was a friendship forged amidst the delights of youth generally: poverty, rivalry, fellowship, and song.

Just as Spenser was familiar, from his own past as a sizar at Cambridge, with the simplicity and servitude that accompany poverty, so too, Harvey, the son of a farmer and rope maker from Saffron-Walden, suffered little demotion in economic rank in the person of the shepherd Hobbinol: "Poverty was indeed Harvey's constant attendant during his life, and even a friendly interpreter like [Moore] Smith suggests that the ascetic life adopted by Harvey, with its emphasis on moderation was probably forced on him by his impecuniosity as well as by his principles" (McLane, 251). If poverty binds men together, so too does political self-preservation, and the two scholars undoubtedly enjoyed their share of youthful rivalry at Cambridge. Spenser could not have made himself too popular by befriending and supporting Harvey, whose general unpopularity and its consequences are well documented.[6]

Spenser and Harvey's own friendship was not free of the sort of rivalry that they experienced with their fellow students. To read what remains of their correspondence is to find ongoing quarrels over principles and disputes over the best possible way of life. A draft of one letter in particular illustrates the nature and tone of these quarrels, and also provides a clear depiction of Harvey the realist. The letter, from which I quoted in chapter 1, was composed with fellow "pastoral" drinking companions at Trinity College where Harvey was now a fellow. Replying to Spenser's musing on times better than their own, Harvey writes:

You suppose it a foolish madd worlde, wherein all thinges ar overrulid by fansye. What greater error? . . . You suppose most of these bodily and sensual pleasures ar to be abandonid as unlawfull and the inwarde contemplative delightes of the minde more zealously to be imbracid as most commendable. Good Lord, you a gentleman, a courtier, an yuthe, and go aboute to revive so owlde and stale a bookishe opinion, dead and buried many hundrid yeares before you or I knewe whether there were any world or noe! You are suer the sensible and ticklinge pleasures of the tastings, feelinge, smellinge, seinge, and hearinge ar very recreative and delectable indeede. Your ether delightes proceedinge of sum strange melancholy conceites and speculative imaginations discursid at large in your fansye and brayne ar but imaginarye and fantasticall delightes, and but for names sake might as well and more trulye be callid the extremist labours and miserabletiste torments under the sunne. (*Letter-Book*, 86)

While the matter treated here contains some philosophic serious-ness, we recognize in the recreative setting of the letter's composi-tion, and in Harvey's bantering tone, the playful nature of pastoral rivalry. We see as well the connection between the subject matter of Harvey-Spenser conversations and Hobbinol-Colin conversa-tions. For what is *The Shepheardes Calender* if not an elaborate dis-course upon the most pleasing and most lasting delights—what is real and what is mere fancy? This question is at the center of every eclogue of the *Calender*, whether it be old versus young in Thenot and Cuddie, sensual versus spiritual in Piers and Palinode, temporal versus eternal in Cuddie and Piers, or all of these in Hobbinol's dia-logue with Colin.

In Harvey's own description of letter-writing, we see that the most serious aim of these extravagant discourses with his corre-spondent is the sustaining and fortifying of their friendship. "Desir-inge continuance of entier friendshipp and owlde acquayntaunce by familiar and good fellowy writinge," Harvey writes: "What are letters amongst frendes but familiar discourses and pleasante con-ferences and what stoick or eremite will bar them of any merri-ments and jests that are not ether merely undecent or simply unhonest." Harvey's desire for continued friendship and his means of sustaining that friendship through mock-serious admonitions and scoldings of his friend are reflected in Hobbinol's efforts in *The Shepheardes Calender* to keep his friend upon pastoral soil. In par-ticular, the manner in which Harvey calls Spenser from fancy down to earth recalls the dialogue of the June Eclogue, where Hobbinol, though seemingly fanciful, makes a case for "bodily and sensual pleasures" as a means toward "contemplative delightes": The "Shepheardes ritch / And fruictfull flocks" find "frendly Faeries, met with many Graces" (June, 21, 23, 25).

As I noted in earlier chapters, any romanticizing of the university world was left to Spenser, who was no longer in it. Spenser's moti-vation may not have been purely nostalgic. As McLane notes, he may have had Harvey's own professional interests in mind in pasto-ralizing Cambridge for his ambitious friend: "To Spenser now in the world of affairs, Cambridge with its opportunities for leisure, scholarship, and poetry no doubt had its appeal as that Paradise which Adam lost. Spenser, too, well aware of Harvey's defects of character that would—and did—hamper his ambition to become another Sir Thomas Smith or Lord Burghley, would be interested in emphasizing the conventional, attractive aspect of the academic life" (244). That Spenser and Harvey shared the joy of song, or poetry, is also born out in their correspondence. Mostly, it would seem that Spenser did the singing, and Harvey provided the critique,[7] and thus it is portrayed in the *Calender*. Colin says:

> Fro thence I durst in derring doe compare
> With shepheards swayne what euer fedde in field:
> And if that Hobbinol right iudgement bare,
> To Pan his owne selfe pype I neede not yield.
>
> (December, l.43–46)

Insofar as he can rely on Hobbinol's good judgment, Colin says, his own songs are as good as Pan's. Such judgment is of course the very kind that won Midas a pair of ass's ears, but the passage suggests the sort of praise that Harvey apparently lavished upon the younger Spenser's work amidst their broader discussions of poetics. Debates over poetry would continue to fill their correspondence, debates probably begun at Cambridge when the two were young. Though "Algrind" and "Roffy" are likely pastoralized versions of Grindal and Master Young, respectively, Harvey is the only pastoralized figure in the *Calender* who positively dates back to Spenser's Cambridge days. That Spenser and Harvey met at Cambridge, and were companions in this environment of youthful fellowship, goes a long way toward explaining why their friendship could withstand differences in principle and temperament. Their friendship was not based merely upon mutual admiration. Nor was it a court-formed alliance that came with political entanglement. It was a college-formed friendship, and as such it had, perhaps, an innocence to it that, when colored by nostalgia, made it a suitable model for the simple rustic companionship of two shepherds.

McLane refers to Spenser's sonnet, "To the right worshipfull M. Gabriell Haruey, my singular good Frend, Doctor of the Lawes," in which Spenser praises Harvey's position of independence in the detached world of the university. Spenser addresses his friend: "Haruey, the happy aboue happiest men, / I read; that sitting like a looker-on / Of this worldes stage . . ." (l.1–3). McLane believes the sonnet may have been "composed at a moment when Spenser coveted his friend's leisure for literary work and freedom from the uncertainty and tyrannous demands of Irish life" (245). There were no doubt many such moments, and it did not take Ireland to produce them. Spenser's longing can be heard long before his departure to a foreign land, when Colin blesses Hobbinol's state in his familiar first lines in the June Eclogue. The contrast between Hobbinol, who belongs to Adam's recovered paradise, and Colin, who must depart it, is the central tension from which the poem derives its energy. The centrality of their relationship to the poem is supported by the other eclogues, in which the same dichotomy of recovery and loss is presented in the dialogues of other shepherds. *The Shepheardes Calender*, therefore, may rightly be described as a poem filled with grief, so long as one understands that the central grief in the poem belongs to Colin Clout, who, with his pastoral companions, mourns the death of his own youth.

The February Eclogue turns us from the mourning of Colin, who has given over the delights of pastoral paradise (complete with "kiddes and cracknelles") for a thwarted love affair, to that of Thenot, whose pastoral paradise has been lost to years of experience in *this* world. In Thenot, we see the pastoral joys through the eyes of one who has long lost them, and who recalls them with a fondness that disrupts the stern admonition he wishes to impart to the young world's child, Cuddie.

Cuddie and Thenot engage in a classic confrontation of youth and age. The two are extremes who, while they appear to have nothing in common, are actually linked together by their opposing views. One image of *festina lente* in the Renaissance was of two reapers, one youthful, the other aged, sharing the labor of carrying a large basket at harvest. Together Cuddie and Thenot comprise just such an image. They are joined by what Berger calls the paradise principle. Having lost paradise, Thenot looks backward to what he has lost. He insists, meanwhile, that any attempt to indulge in life's joys is frivolous. Cuddie's code is pleasure. He looks forward to whatever enjoyment might come next, and finds any attempt to call him away from it to be but the foolish grumblings of an old man. Yet, as Berger points out, the two shepherds "are more in agreement than they know" ("Aging Boy," 36)—the one, after all, lives for what the other has lost.

The eclogue opens with the young "Herdsmans boye," complaining of the "bitter blasts" of winter, which presumably have

interrupted his pleasure. Embedded in Thenot's practical response
to Cuddie's complaint is his understanding of the world's ways:

> Must not the world wend in his common course
> From good to badd, and badde to worse,
> From worse vnto that is worst of all,
> And then returne to his former fall?
>
> (1.11–14)

No talk of eternal spring here—the world has its natural seasons,
and the wise swain abides by them. He, of course, is such a swain
and has never once complained:

> Selfe haue I worne out thrise threttie yeares,
> Some in much joy, many in many teares:
> Yet neuer complained of cold nor heate,
> of Sommers flame, nor of Winters threat.
>
> (1.17–20)

"Do the many sad years follow because the joys lasted too short a
time?" asks Berger (29). His suggestion is that within Thenot's
boastful account of his own life is a hint of nostalgic lament with
which all of his speeches are laced. What we find beneath Thenot's
posture of the stern, scolding elder, in other words, is a man who
misses his youth. "It becomes clear," says Berger, "that keeping in
touch with youth is as important as putting it down, that putting it
down is a way to stay in touch" (30).

Keeping in touch with youth, as I have argued throughout this
chapter, is what the ekphrastic promise of pastoral is all about. *The
Shepheardes Calender* clearly illustrates this idea in tracing Colin's
movement, and eventual departure, from the world of youth. That
Thenot's reminiscence in this eclogue takes the form of resentment
does not lessen its nostalgic content. Just as Colin recalls his careless years even as he leaves them behind—indeed, so that he *can*
leave them behind—so Thenot reprimands Cuddie's youthful carelessness, and in so doing, re-creates in images that which he has
long since lost.

Not surprisingly, the boastful Thenot is bothered most by the arrogance he sees in Cuddie and his companions, who, unknowing of
what the future holds, are completely careless:

> . . . crowing in pypes made of greene corne,
> You thinken to be Lords of the yeare.
> But eft, when ye count you freed from feare,
> Comes the breme winter with chamfred browes,
> Full of wrinckles and frostie furrowes.
>
> (1.40–44)

Man is servant to the seasons, not the other way around, and the young swain with his pipe is no exception to this rule. Thenot's admonition here is more than a common notion. He speaks, it would seem, with the backing of experience. The frivolity of Cuddie and his companions would not bother Thenot so if he himself did not know at firsthand the penalty for being frivolous. Thenot, we may suppose, despite his elder boasting, was once a young man caught by winter. As Berger explains: "Thenot's attachment to the philosophy of waste, and his stoic counsel, seem intimately associated with his attachment to the joys of youth, his bitterness at their early, perhaps unexpected loss" (29).

To recognize this paradox in Thenot is to better understand Colin and the general movement of the *Calender*. As Thenot's stoic counsel to Cuddie cannot be separated from his feelings of loss, just so Colin will mock his own youth even as he reluctantly parts with it. What caused Thenot's unexpected loss of youth we can surmise from the above admonition he delivers to Cuddie. Assuming that he speaks from his own experience, the old swain seems to have aged as suddenly as Colin imagines himself to have, and his words clearly foreshadow Colin's winter departure in the December Eclogue. The source of Thenot's sudden aging is the same that has caused Colin's current misfortunes: "a stormy darte" that "pricks the harte."

That Thenot was attached to the joys of youth, replete with Rosalinds, as Cuddie is now, suggests something about those joys— namely, that they are not entirely frivolous. Berger finds Thenot voicing essentially two sentiments in his debate with Cuddie. First, youth is careless and spends itself on trifles, and second, youth is foolish in its clinging to joys that it must soon lose. As Berger points out, this latter sentiment "implies that the joys are more than mere trifles" (30). Thenot can only persuade with half strength since he admonishes Cuddie not to lose himself in the joys to which he himself was more than likely lost. The distance of time seems to have taught him that the joys of youth are more than mere trifles.

He regards them as folly "not because they are evil but because they are short-lived and it is painful to lose them" (34). Thus, he does not condemn pastoral song, but rather pokes fun at the "crowing" of Cuddie and his companions. Since the tale he tells is one he learned in his youth, we assume that he was once cautioned in the very manner he is admonishing Cuddie, and that he was well acquainted with the pastoral joy of fellowship. And when he admonishes Cuddie, "All that is lent to love, wyll be lost," he speaks as well from his own experience of stormy darts. What Thenot preaches, Colin experiences, and Cuddie ignores.

Thenot, more than Cuddie, knows the value of what Cuddie has, but his knowing yields him little joy. Thenot has the knowledge without the delights. Cuddie enjoys the delights without knowledge. He indulges in the pleasures youth offers him, but shows little awareness of their real value, a fact that is readily apparent in his boasting. Both men are, as Berger says, "partly right, partly wrong, and each being incomplete, needs the other" (36). Needing each other or not, however, neither has patience with the other. Thenot cannot bear Cuddie's careless action, and Cuddie, in turn, cannot even bear to let Thenot finish his tale of woe. When the young Brere sees that "the byting frost nipt his stalke dead" and "The watrie wette weighed downe his head" (l.232), and he is left in the dirt to be trod on by cattle, Cuddie stops the old man's story.

This disrupted dialogue ends, or rather stops, amidst a yoking of seeming opposites that characterizes the entire *Calender*. The young shepherd and the old are united by the paradise the one enjoys and the other has lost. A similar harmony of discords (Berger calls them "unities-in-polarity"), can be found in each of the eclogues. Just so, as I have noted, we find the pastoral delights throughout the eclogues in essentially two places: among those who enjoy them presently, and among those who recollect them as part of their past. Between these goes Colin Clout, hastening slowly, toward his formal forsaking of the pastoral delights of youth in December. The *Calender*'s dialogues provide detailed descriptions of those delights even while choreographing Colin's movement toward forsaking them. These detailed descriptions, I argue, stem from Spenser's own vision, which is colored by a nostalgic remembrance of his own youth, most notably in the academic world of Cambridge. This remembrance prevents him from scorning the delights that Colin leaves behind. He may regard them as a sort of folly, and yet, like Thenot, he does so not because they are evil, but because they are short-lived, and he experiences some pain at their loss.

By April, Colin is notable by his absence. We find Hobbinol "complayning . . . of that boyes great misaduenture in Loue, whereby his mynd was alienate and with drawen not onely from him who moste loued him, but also from all former delightes and studies, aswell in pleasaunt pyping, as conning ryming and singing, and other his laudable exercises" (Argument, April). Here in the argument we are provided with an inventory of the joys Colin has forsaken. The eclogue opens when Thenot[8] greets Hobbinol with the conventional inquiry seeking an explanation for the sorrowful swain's sad visage:

> Tell me good Hobbinol, what garres thee greete?
> What? hath some Wolfe thy tender Lambes ytorne?
> Or is thy Bagpype broke, that soundes so sweete?
> Or art thou of thy loued lasse forlorne?
>
> (l.1–4)

The tears that trickle down Hobbinol's cheek "like April shoure" are not caused by a faithless lass, nor by his broken pipe. These catastrophes are the source of Colin's sorrow, whose unfaithfulness, in turn, causes Hobbinol's. Hobbinol complains to Thenot of his injury at having lost Colin's affection: "So nowe fayre Rosalind hath bredde hys smart, / So now his frend is chaunged for a frenne"[9] (27–28).

Hobbinol then turns to the general loss caused by Colin's misadventure in love—namely, the loss of Colin's songs and the merriment they provided the pastoral circle. Colin has shut out from his mind the "delightes and studies" over which he formerly reigned: piping, making rhymes, and singing. Again, it should be emphasized that Colin has not forsaken these delights in hopes of something higher. He has not abandoned pastoral rhyming to become a heroic poet. He is hurt by love. His eyes are bent toward the past, and his mind is withdrawn.

That Hobbinol and Thenot sit down "shrowded in thys shade alone" tells us that, for Hobbinol, pastoral fellowship remains with or without Colin, but the song of Eliza that Hobbinol sings is one of Colin's. And, as one who has lost a part of paradise, Hobbinol recollects nostalgically the time when his friend first composed the song: "Which once he made, as by a spring he laye, / And tuned it vnto the Waters fall" (35–36). The subject of the song is suggestive of Colin's future vocation of epic poet, even while it gives tribute to his former pastoral manner of singing.

Nostalgic reminiscence likewise colors the beginning of the May Eclogue, where we are presented with two "pastors," who, prompted by the season, recollect youthful delights. One does so with envy and the other with pity. Critics, following the prescription of E. K. ("under the persons of Piers and Palinode, be represented two forms of pastoures or Ministers, or the protestant and the Catholique"), have generally emphasized the religious conflict within this eclogue. Thus Piers is generally seen as the allegorical model of the perfect minister of the Anglican flock and Palinode as the unrestrained Roman. Like Thenot and Cuddie, however, these two pastors are unified even in their opposing views, and their differences should not be exaggerated. To begin with, they do share a fellowship between them. As Cullen notes, if Piers believed Palinode was "a thoroughly corrupt shepherd like those he denounces, he would quite clearly be inconsistent in keeping fellowship with him" (45). Palinode is comic in his dreamy yearnings, which send his "heart after the pype to daunce" when the parade of shepherds goes by "eche one with his mayd." The strength of his argument, though, lies not in dreaminess, but in practical suggestion:

> Is not thilke the mery moneth of May
> When loue lads masken in fresh aray?
> How falles it then, we no merrier be,
> Ylike as others, girt in gawdy greene?
>
> (l.1–4)

Perhaps Palinode's answer lies in the fact that he is not one of the "Youthes folke" who now "flocken in euery where." But to him it is not a matter of age. Those who do not join in the "pleasaunce" are the ones who are lost in a dream: "Such merimake holy Saints doth queme, / But we here sytten as drownd in a dreme" (15–16).

What to Palinode is a practical, or at least a natural, response is to Piers a frivolous temptation, and like the aged Thenot he claims to pity those who are lost in such sports as gathering May baskets while "letting their sheepe runne at large." Clearly the argument between the two pastors concerns the proper way to shepherd a flock. The ecclesiastical allegory is thick enough so as not to be missed, but on a more fundamental level the eclogue, like all the others, concerns the delights that comprise the pastoral world. Colin's mind is "alienate" of such delights, and Piers would count this as a good sign. Palinode, however, would recognize, as Hobbinol does, that Colin is "drownd in a dreme." He would likely tell Colin the same thing he tells Piers: "Sicker now I see thou speakest of spight / All for thou lackest somedele their delight" (55–56).[10] Your righteousness, in other words, is seeded in regret. The response, of course, is that your carelessness is rooted in desire, or in Piers's words, "thou art a worldes childe."

That neither Palinode nor Piers is entirely right in his point of view concerning the pastoral delights is shown in the next eclogue when Colin, having forsaken the delights, is steeped in misery, and Hobbinol, the proverbial harbinger of those delights, is unable to console him. Much has already been said in this chapter regarding the June Eclogue. I do not wish to repeat myself here, only point to the eclogue's significance. For, besides being the halfway point structurally in the twelve eclogues, it is central in other ways. It is the only eclogue in which Colin and Hobbinol appear together, a circumstance of some significance, since we know by this point in the *Calender* not only about the friendship between the two shepherds but the conflict as well. Hobbinol is child of a world that Colin has begun to forsake. As such he is unable to enter Hobbinol's paradise, a *locus amoenus* of song and fellowship unfit for Colin, who forsakes the company and judgment of his fellow shepherds: "But pyping lowe in shade of lowly groue, / I play to please me selfe, all be it ill" (71–72). Alone in this shade is where we will find Colin in December before his departure. The joy of pastoral fellowship requires a companion, yet, as the *Calender* opens with Colin alone, so too it will close.

Before Colin's departure in December, however, he participates a final time in the fellowship of the pastoral world within the *Calender*. In the November Eclogue we see that Colin has begun to understand the nature of the pastoral world of which he is the center. Though seemingly inconsolable himself, he offers, at Thenot's prompting, the conventional consolation of elegiac for Lobbin, who weeps for Dido, his dead beloved. Whatever embedded reference may be here to Leicester, the Dudley family, or Elissa herself, we can accept E. K.'s claim that "the personage is secrete" and concentrate instead on the manner in which the theological truth of resurrection combines with pastoral ekphrasis as Colin's song (like the *Calender* itself, which is now nearing its completion) offers to preserve in image that which has been lost. Colin's song for Dido moves by the repetition of a still image, "O heavie herse," and still words, "O carefull verse," until it arrives by sudden Christian logic at an alternate image: "O happy herse / O joyfull verse."

Berger regards Colin's elegiac song of Dido in the same way that Dr. Johnson views Milton's "Lycidas": as a matter of mere convention. "Colin's motive for singing the elegy," he claims, "is no more personal than Thenot's: decorum is the criterion in terms of which he chooses his selection; he sings a sad song not for Dido but for the onset of winter" ("Aging Boy," 38). That elegy is appropriate to November is true enough. However, the unfounded assertion that Colin is merely performing a proper set piece to fit the month unnecessarily trivializes, I believe, Spenser's use of pastoral. Colin's own mood is one of grief, and there is nothing to suggest that he is not actually singing on behalf of Lobbin's deceased bride and offering to Lobbin the comfort of which he is sorely in need.

Hamilton, while assigning more significance to the song, seems to regard it largely as Colin's own private uncovering of the Christian assurance of resurrection, which, "together with the aspiration in October to cast off his shepherd's weeds, brings him to the resolution of the final eclogue when he lays down the oaten pipe and emerges as England's heroic poet" ("Argument," 175). The assurance of another world, in other words, prompts Colin to forsake his present one in favor of what to Hamilton, presumably, is the more spiritually significant task of the heroic poet.

This theological focus upon Colin's role disregards the basic human comfort he offers to Lobbin, and depicts Colin as one who sings of the destruction of death and the joy of eternal life solely for his own benefit. That Colin shows signs of a Christian hope that replaces his previous despair is true. He has, as he says, "learnd (a lesson derely bought) / That nys on earth assurance to be sought" (l.156–57). Yet his news of resurrection is contained within an image of the passing of Dido:

> But maugre death, and dreaded sisters deadly spight,
> And gates of hel, and fyrie furies forse:
> She hath the bonds broke of eternall night,
> Her soule vnbodied of the burdenous corpse.

> (l.162–65)

Colin has had to look beyond himself and beyond his own sad circumstance in order to see the bonds of eternal night broken, an event that necessarily lessens the previously unrelenting shadow of his own misery.

Colin's own cause for grieving pales next to Lobbin's. He has lamented the loss of a beloved, who, ungrateful from the start, is now paired with another. He has not only refused to sing, but has refused even the consolation of song. Lobbin, on the other hand, is a shepherd who has lost a faithful love to death, and requires the consolation of song. That Colin, when urged by Thenot to sing, agrees to do so indicates that he has not yet forsaken the pastoral world nor the consolation it can provide. Colin might well have broken his silence with a song cataloging his own sorrow. Instead, he sings "O Lobb, *thy* losse no longer lament" [italics mine]. The pipe, which in the woodcuts of January, June, and December lies broken on the ground, is, in the November woodcut, restored and in the able and accomodating hands of Colin. In January his own hurt caused him to smash the pipe. Now in November another's hurt prompts him to pick it up again. As Rosenmeyer observes, the November Eclogue is a case in which "the accent is on the restorative character of *otium*" (113). Neither swain, however, is to be healed of his grief by pastoral song, which is but a soothing, not a healing, agent. What Colin has accomplished in his song, and what Spenser is about to in his, is the pastoral act of ekphrastic preservation.

In December, we are returned to the unpastoral silhouette of a solitary swain. The eclogue's argument tells us that in this solitary state Colin,

> weary of his former wayes . . . proportioneth his life to the foure seasons of the yeare, comparing hys youthe to the spring time, when he was fresh and free from loues follye. His manhoode to the sommer, which he sayth, was consumed with greate heate and excessiue drouth caused throughe a Comet or blasinge starre, by which he meaneth loue. . . . His riper yeares hee resembleth to an unseasonable harueste wherein the fruites fall ere they be rype. His latter age to winters chyll and frostie season, now drawing neare to his last ende.

As we read through the seasons of Colin's life, we are reminded of what we already know. First, that it was love that took away his youth and its accompanying delights: "Loue they him called, that gaue me checkmate / But better mought they haue behote him Hate. / Tho gan my louely Spring bid me farewel" (l.53–55). Colin recalls the summer spent in "vnkindly heate" and the fruitlessness that followed:

The flattring fruite is fallen to grownd before,
And rotted, ere they were halfe mellow ripe:
My haruest wast, my hope away dyd wipe.

(1.105–7)

Soon "Delight is layd abedde, and pleasure past" (137) then, "Winter is come . . . And after Winter dreerie death dost hast" (143–44), or at least thoughts of death. This awareness of death is not new to Colin. His experience with Rosalind showed him his mortality and taught him the end of things. Here at last in December, dies a self that has been ailing throughout the *Calender*, the youthful Colin of the pleasant pipe.

Colin has erred in the exact fashion described by Thenot to Cuddie, the blunder of eternal youth. Unlike Thenot, however, Colin's complaint is not shrouded in a cloak of elder wisdom, but spoken with undisguised bitterness (yet one more indication that Colin is not very old). His bitterness is the bitterness of loss. Hamilton says that "the whole eclogue is a formal retraction of youthful vanities" ("The Grene Path," 19), as though Colin were obliged to disavow his former life. I do not believe this to be the case, for beneath Colin's bitterness—and not very far beneath—is the same ingredient that lies beneath Thenot's admonishing and Piers's preaching: a nostalgic longing for that which is past. Colin has not of a sudden become Thenot or Piers. He is neither very old nor very clerical, and to read this final eclogue as a sort of Ecclesiastes is to disregard the tone of personal sadness with which his recollection is filled.

Colin's departure from the world of the *Calender*, while necessary, is not necessarily a rejection of pastoral itself. The final lines of the *Calender*, in which Colin bids adieu to the delights he has known, are filled more with reluctance than rejection. Depiction of the pastoral joys through the eyes of loss, which we have seen throughout the *Calender*, appropriately brings the *Calender* to a close:

> Adieu delightes, that lulled me asleepe,
> Adieu my deare, whose loue I bought so deare:
> Adieu my little Lambes and loued sheepe,
> Adieu ye Woodes that oft my witnesse were:
>   Adieu good Hobbinol, that was so true,
> Tell Rosalind, her Colin bids her adieu.
>
> (December, 151–56)[11]

E. K. assigns a particular importance to these departing lines by providing the reader a line-by-line explication of the stanza. "Adiew delights," he tells the reader, "is a conclusion of all. Where in six verses he comprehendeth briefly all that was touched in this booke." The lines contain, in other words, a sum of all that has comprised the *Calender*—namely, the pastoral delights that Colin must now leave behind, the most important of which is his friendship with Hobbinol.

The first verse describes these delights that lulled Colin to sleep, or kept him at peace. E. K. rightfully calls these the delights of youth generally. In the second line he bids adieu to Rosalind, the dear whose love he bought so dear. This love, as we have seen, was bought at the price of all the other delights. As he says earlier in the eclogue, better might they call it hate. In the third line he recalls, not just the task of shepherding, but his little lambs, and loved sheep. In so doing he demonstrates a fondness for the vocation he is leaving behind. In quitting his life as shepherd he leaves behind as well the joy of poverty/simplicity that he has shared with his fellow swains. He next bids adieu to the woods, which were often his witness. The woods have been more than woods; they have been the place for song. Long before they listened to his complaints about Rosalind, they served as the pleasant gathering place for him and his fellow swains. As shepherding has yielded the time for song, the woods have supplied the place. What Colin bids goodbye to in this line is the joy of the *locus amoenus*. Finally, he bids adieu to his best friend and fellow shepherd, Hobbinol, whom he has most recently hurt by his refusal to sing, and the denial of his fellowship. Here he says adieu to the pastoral joy of fellowship and the accompanying joy of friendship. That he values this love above that of Rosalind's is indicated in the final line, when he tells Hobbinol to bid adieu to Rosalind for him. Rosalind's love was bought, he tells us, at a dear price. Yet he departs this world without that love. He can bring with him, instead, the love of Hobbinol, "that was so true."

In the ninth canto of Book VI of *The Faerie Queene*, with his epic labor nearly fulfilled and the excuse of an "aged" Colin no longer needed, Spenser restores the youthful version of himself to the center of a world far surpassing the world of the *Calender* in its delights. That Colin is now the pastoral shepherd whom we have heard of but never seen (he stepped into the January Eclogue disgruntled and we rely on the word of Hobbinol to assure us that

Colin was once happy) is exhibited not only in his shrill piping and its happy results, but in the prolonged conversation that follows the characteristic smashing of his pipe.

He and the pseudo-shepherd Calidore enter into conversation, which, like the other pastoral joys Calidore has learned from Meliboeus, is reminiscent of the academic campus, and, here again, Calidore is the pupil. Colin, after his initial tantrum, educates the disruptive knight on the meaning of the Graces. Following this, Calidore apologizes: "But gentle Shepheard pardon thou my shame, / Who rashly sought that, which I mote not see" (29.6–7). The two, thus reconciled, do not depart, but rather remain in the *locus amoenus*, and the vanished ecstasy of love and song is replaced by the *otium* of fellowship and conversation:

> In such discourses they together spent
> Long time, as fit occasion forth them led;
>   With which the Knight him selfe did much content,
>   And with delight his greedy fancy fed,
> Both of his words, which we with reason red;
> And also of the place, whose pleasures rare
> With such regard his sences rauished,
> That thence he had no will away to fare,
> But wisht, that with that shepheard he mote dwelling share.
>
> (x.30)

This "fit occasion" is made so largely by the place, which is apart from the greater world. As for time, it dissolves. Colin's fanciful sport with the dancing maidens had risen with the notes of his pipe to a brief height, interrupted before its climax. The discourse between these two men, however, is prolonged for a "long time," and Calidore, who many have seen as a representation of Philip Sidney, is caught up in the words of Colin, with "no will away to fare." Their conversation erodes any concerns of time. Here is the *otium* that was left behind by Colin at the end of the *Calender*. Richard Helgerson is justified in calling Mount Acidale "the center of Spenser's retreat," for the above stanza contains as full and meaningful a description of the delight of youthful fellowship as is found anywhere in Spenser. When Fletcher and others imitated Spenser in their pastorals, they looked as much to these cantos of *The Faerie Queene* as to *The Shepheardes Calender*.

The *otium* shared between Calidore and Colin Clout is interrupted, predictably, by love. Colin's lass has vanished with the Graces, but Calidore's awaits him back in the open fields. "But [for] that enuenimd sting, the which of yore, / His poysnous point deepe fixed in his hart" (31.1–2), Calidore might have dwelt longer with Colin, but his wound calls him—like a whale—from this *locus amoenus* of the pastoral back to the world of romance. Calidore takes leave of the gentle swain and "backe returned to his rusticke wonne, / Where his faire Pastorella did remaine" (32.1–2). As Hamilton points out in his edition of *The Faerie Queene*, the simile of the wounded whale is startling, "for the whale goes to its death" (694). However, when we recall the pastoral connection of love to death, and Colin's own "death" to his youthful self in *The Shepherdes Calender*, the simile is meaningfully appropriate. Calidore's return, after the defeat of a troop of brigands and other obstacles, will result in a consummation of his love in marriage, and this, as I discussed in chapter 2, means a "death" to pastoral. Calidore will exchange his present, temporary *otium* for *negotium*. The delights of the pastoral world, soon to be lost, will become something fondly recollected.

Fond recollection, I suggest, was the perspective of Spenser himself, who, finishing work on *The Faerie Queene*, was now even further away from the pastoral joys he had enjoyed during his youth at Cambridge when, at points perhaps, "he had no will away to fare." Like Calidore, however, Spenser's quest was of the heroic nature, and *The Faerie Queene*, his heroic work. Calidore returns to the world of the court with a bride who, as it turns out, is also of that world. Spenser, on the other hand, less resolved than his knight, leaves heroic questing to its inevitable mutability and returns to less public enterprises in *Amoretti* and *Epithalamion*, and back to the pastoral in *Colin Cloutes Come Home Againe*. Of these works, Helgerson observes that Spenser "comes home to the pastoral, the personal and the amorous. That these are also among his most resonant works, among those that engage the cosmic shape of things most confidently, is testimony to the poetic richness of that home. Whatever the poet's obligations to the public world, it is in this private realm that he finds the source of his inspiration" (907). The private, the personal, and the pastoral, I have argued, are what Spenser left behind twenty some years earlier when he departed the gardens of Pembroke College determined to become England's poet. Only after preserving this maturing version of himself ekphrastically within the confines of *The Shepheardes Calender* could

Spenser turn to the greater world where the gardens were cultivated by more powerful hands, and the *otium* of conversation replaced by the *negotium* of public advancement. Friendship is as scarce as it is suspect in such a world, where each utterance is indeed one of power. It is little wonder that Spenser wrote to Harvey at Cambridge in such a reminiscent manner. What Spenser had discovered by the time he wrote *Colin Cloutes Come Home Againe* is something many critics still have not—namely, that the court could never be successfully described in pastoral terms. Thankfully Spenser, in composing his *Calender*, had in his imagination recollection of a more collegiate place.

5

"Ungrateful Chame!"

IN 1619, THE AUTHORITIES AT CAMBRIDGE UNIVERSITY EXPERIENCED
some anxiety as Parliament debated a bill ordering the drainage of
Cambridgeshire fens. Such an action might endanger what the university sought to preserve, "the navigation of the River Cam"
(Cooper and Cooper, 3.131). The river, memorialized in Spenser's
lengthy river pageant in Book IV of *The Faerie Queene*, was
formed from the convergence of several small brooks and streams,
below which junction it was called either the Grant or the Cam,
until "it traced its courses among the colleges through Cambridge,"
where it became known simply as the Cam (Osgood, "Spencer's
Rivers," 80).[1] Here the Cam became part of the separate world of
the university that we have been examining, and here Phineas
Fletcher, during his stay at Cambridge, memorialized its shores in
his *Piscatorie Eclogues*, a work of seven eclogues that transfers the
pastoral values he inherited from Virgil and Spenser[2] into a piscatory world he adopted from Theocritus's Eclogue XXI and from the
Italian poet Jacopo Sannazaro. The result is a world of fisher swains
casting out their nets along the shores of the River Chame.

Fletcher's epic, *The Purple Island*, has long been recognized as
providing a bridge between *The Faerie Queene* and *Paradise Lost*.
"The interest and the glory of the Fletchers," C. V. Wedgwood observes, "is to provide the link between the two greatest epic poets
of the English language. It is in their work that the gigantic and
dissimilar geniuses of Spenser and Milton are brought, for a moment, edge to edge" (54).[3] No one as yet, however, has examined
the extent to which Fletcher's *Eclogues* provided a similar link between the green world of Spenser's *Calender* and the blue world of
Milton's "Lycidas." The general and specific influences of Fletcher's piscatory world become apparent when we give full consideration to the university world from which all three of these poets and
their pastorals came.

100

Evolving out of *The Shepheardes Calender* and anticipating "Lycidas," Fletcher's world is the most overt transference of the university world into the pastoral. In a frame of piscatory bliss, with its accompanying joys of fellowship, poverty, and rivalry, Fletcher records, among other things, his own, as well as his father's, failed attempt to secure a permanent fellowship at Cambridge. This overt use of academic allegory, which Spenser successfully avoided, tells us, nonetheless, something of the nature of the *Calender*, which Fletcher imitated, and "Lycidas," which he influenced. As a poet, Fletcher characteristically did overtly what Spenser had accomplished with far greater subtlety. His *Eclogues*, therefore, reveal, if somewhat glaringly, the sort of academic ingredients that make English pastoral English.

Though not published until 1633, most of the *Piscatorie Eclogues* was composed between 1604 and 1614, a period Fletcher spent off and on in residence at Cambridge University, where he found himself at the center of a literary clique pleased to regard itself as Spenserian.[4] With a prompting from Theocritus's Eclogue XXI and the *Piscatorial Eclogues* of the Italian Jacopo Sannazaro as a precedent, Fletcher set about creating a work of seven eclogues in which we find young swains casting their nets along the deceptively calm shores of the River Cam. In his 1984 article "The Latin and English Eclogues of Phineas Fletcher: Sannazaro's *Piscatoria* among the Britons," Lee Piepho observed that "the inwardness and detachment from place evident throughout [Fletcher's] eclogues especially prevented him from penetrating to the imaginative center of Sannazaro's piscatory world . . . In his *Piscatorie Eclogues*," Piepho notes, "Phineas Fletcher, for better or worse, tried another way" (468). In my present investigation of Fletcher's *Eclogues*, I wish to add to Professor Piepho's observations that the "other way" chosen by Fletcher was the way he had inherited from Spenser and in his turn passed on to Milton. It was never to the imaginative center of Sannazaro that Fletcher sought to penetrate, but to that of his English master in the pastoral. The inwardness and detachment from place that Piepho rightly observes in Fletcher has its English origins in Spenser and characterizes no other work so much as Milton's "Lycidas." Mimicking the reluctant departure of Colin Clout from the fields of Spenser's *Shepheardes Calender* and anticipating the watery loss of the uncouth swain, Fletcher's *Piscatorie Eclogues* provided a bridge between the pastoral worlds of these two more prominent poets who, like himself, spent the latter part of their youth in residence along the River Cam.

Fletcher's assumption of the pastoral pseudonym Thirsil and his consequent choice of the pastoral eclogue form established him in the, by then, conventional Greek-Latin-English manner of preparing oneself to write an epic poem. His decision to shift from the field to the riverbank, while innovative to English poetry, was not entirely eccentric given the historic company of Theocritus and Sannazaro. By turning from the more traditional world of the shepherd to the less familiar world of the fisher swain, Fletcher freed himself, in part, from one of his greatest poetic weaknesses, that of obvious imitation of his predecessor, Spenser. Here in this new world, he would need new imagery. The pipes could stay, but nets would replace staffs, overhanging rocks substitute for shaded groves, and boats be gained or lost instead of land. The piscatory world, however, posed great problems for an English poet. Before examining specific eclogues, therefore, it is worth our while to consider the novelty of their appearance upon otherwise purely pastoral English soil.

The flourishing of the pastoral genre in England had at least something to do with physical environs. If ever a land was ripe, at least from its windows and doorways, for songs surrounding the activity of herding, it was sixteenth-century England. Anglicizing Theocritus's Arcadian fields could be accomplished without straining the imagination of English readers. As for the songs of the angler, that was another matter. The fisherman's world, even as an artificial construct, seems to contradict any notions of the idyllic. In the first place, the primary task of the fisherman, unlike that of the shepherd, is the taking of life. With his hooks and nets he is perhaps more akin to the hunter. It is with a falconer and a hunter, for example, that the happy angler discourses in Izaak Walton's *Complete Angler*. Secondly, and more critically, the sea, especially in these early days of navigation, poses a great threat to the fisherman's own life. "The seas," Spenser proclaims, "doe in the spoile of life delight" (*FQ*, IV.xii.6.9), and he goes on to depict as much in Book III, where the very sea to which Britomart makes her lament becomes Florimell's place of imprisonment rather than refuge. Likewise, ocean waters, while they can serve as a source of food, can serve also as the source of invasion and a place for battle. As early as in the Theocritan-influenced novel, *Daphnis and Chloe* (third century A.D.), the shore serves, not as a home for simple fishermen, but as a landing place for invading brigands. The world of pastoral romance that Spenser creates in Book VI is wrecked by the violence of such sea invaders, who also kill Melobius, Pastorella's father and the model shepherd. Add to this danger nature's own storms and violence, which are always more unpredictable and hazardous on the sea than on the land, and the possibility of piscatory bliss, which Theocritus depicts with very little detail, begins to look more and more precarious.

Alexander Pope was the first, and as far as I know the only, poet to fault the sea as an inappropriate setting for pastoral poetry. Pope was merely expressing critically what his Renaissance predecessors had demonstrated by their avoidance of pastoral seascapes. Petrarch had established the sea as a metaphor for the precarious and potentially fatal nature of love. The English poets, gazing out across gray ocean waters from the cliffs of Dover, were only too willing to believe him. Beginning with Wyatt's translation of "My Galley," seafaring began to rival hunting as the most popular English vehicle for conveying the hazards of the heart. When Shakespeare declared in Sonnet 116 that love was "the star to every wandring bark," he may have found a fond and familiar place in people's hearts, but few consider just what a radical declaration this is in a sixteenth-century sonnet. Up until that point, love was what had caused barks to wander, and wasn't above dashing them against the rocks and drowning the ill-fated passengers within.

Over and over again in the course of *The Faerie Queene*, Spenser uses such wandering barks at sea to describe his characters separated from truth and love. One of the most vivid examples comes in Book III when Britomart makes a Petrarchan address to the "Huge sea of sorrow" (iv.8), calling Love the "lewd Pilot" of her "feeble vessell" (iv.9). For all her figurative complaining, however, she remains solidly on the ground while Florimell, forsaken of the lover whom Britomart wounds, finds herself quite literally adrift at sea in a swelling "cock-bote" about to be raped by a lecherous fisherman (viii.35). When she is rescued from this circumstance by Proteus, "Shepheard of the seas of yore" (viii.30.1), she is scarcely any better off.[5] Nothing, it seems, can go well at sea in the nautical uncertainty of English poetry.

Fletcher was certainly mindful of the sea as the chief claimer of Petrarchan hearts and minds and, steeped devotedly in Spenser's poetry, he did not dare bring the idyllic seascapes of Jacopo Sannazaro across the English Channel. The sublime salt waters of southern Italy may have served a Neapolitan's nostalgic longing for youth and idyllic conversation, but this vast consumer of evil armadas had no such place in the inland English imagination fifteen degrees to the north.

Fletcher therefore kept his fisher swains safely inland. He kept them, as it were, on campus—along the banks of the peaceful, as well as unfishable, River Cam, whose waters, at least from a nautical point of view, were the safest in the British Isles. This setting, besides providing safe "pastoral" harbor,[6] served Fletcher's particular allegorical purpose. Using the inherent rivalry of the fishing profession (i.e., competition for boats, waters, and fish), he created several life-at-Cambridge pieces that begin with his father's ill fortune at Cambridge and record as well his own complaints and subsequent departure from Chamus's shores. Since nymphs inhabit the waves as well as shaded groves, Fletcher was also able to include the traditional love complaints in his eclogues.

Nevertheless, the fact remains that despite the Cam's geographical and conventional conveniences, Fletcher's only literary model for piscatory verse was the distant Neapolitan whom he lists among the sages in *The Purple Island*:

> And now of late th' Italian fisher-swain
> Sits on the shore to watch his trembling line;
> There teaches rocks and prouder seas to plain
> By Nesis fair, and fairer Mergiline:
> While his thinne net, upon his oars twin'd
> With wanton strife catches the Sunne, and winde,
> Which still do slip away, and still remain
> behinde.
>
> (I.13.l.1–7)[7]

Having set to the task of anglicizing this angler, Fletcher did not use his lines to "catch the Sunne and winde" like his Italian predecessor. The most immediate difference between Fletcher and his Italian influence is that the world that Sannazaro creates is decidedly more piscatory. Fletcher, like Sannazaro, pastoralized the world of fish, but he did so in a decidedly English fashion.[8] He gathered images from Sannazaro's piscatory world, but he inherited his Virgilian themes, motifs, and images chiefly through Spenser. Thus, he looked to Sannazaro with a sensibility already shaped largely by Spenser, and with an imagination already determined to depict his personal experiences in the academic and ecclesiastical worlds he inhabited. While Sannazaro detailed the material ingredients of the fisherman's world, Fletcher infused his fisher swains with a spiritual and academic dimension that "detached" them from material detail.

The result is that Fletcher's riverbank world is more "pastoralized" (I would say more *English*), more deliberately artificial, than Sannazaro's seaside world, which, for all its Virgilian conventions, is very much a world of fish. The Neapolitan poet spent more time by the sea than his English imitator, whose waterfront experience was presumably confined almost entirely to strolling along the Cam and perhaps the banks of London's Thames. In some of the more graphic lines of Sannazaro one is likely to see (and even smell) fish, as a sample passage demonstrates:

> And while with their fires nearby the others are lighting the familiar bays and fishy flats, or far away are drawing the captive fishes and the linen nets to shore, he [Lycon] is meditating his songs through the dark of night.[9]

Sannazaro's swains, while infused with a poetic dimension, are clearly fishermen, and are—long after Colins and Hobbinols have left the fields with Phoebus's descent—surrounded by the elements of their vocation—the fires, the flats and the nets, and nightfall itself. Even Sannazaro's storms, while they are an occasion for song and fellowship, threaten in a way that Fletcher's do not:

> *Celadon.* Tell me (for the storms at Basuli, if Aegon told me true, held you prisoner, Mopus, for twelve days) what you, what Chromis the while, what your Iolas did, while the South Wind lords it over the sea, while the wave murmurs. . . .
>
> *Mopsus.* What should our Muses do in the unwelcome leisure, O Celadon? For it was impossible then with safety to try for mussels among the rocks, or for the eight-footed crab. Now the stones were guarding the fragile fishing skiff on dry ground and the thin nets were hanging over the long oars. At our feet our hooks and delicate baskets were lying, and fishing rods and wheels and labyrinth made of wicker work.[10]

The swains in Sannazaro's world are, like the delicate baskets and fragile labyrinth surrounding them, entirely vulnerable to the lord-ing-over of the South Wind. They do not pause for an afternoon rain shower, but take refuge for twelve days, during which "unwelcome leisure" they talk of a fleet of young men who sailed forth with their king after the wars. Trusting their lives "to the unknown waves of Ocean," the fleet met with an ill fate, and the blue-eyed Britons, he tells us, "whenever the ocean tide recedes . . . capture the fish [i.e., sailors' bodies] left stranded on the shore."

Such morbid detail has no place in Fletcher's Spenserian *Eclogues*, where the swains face no threat from the stylized storm that interrupts their fishing. In Eclogue II, for example, Myrtilus and Dorus sit "idle on the shore" while "stormy windes, and waves intestine spite / Impatient rage of sail, or bending oare." Unable to fish, the two put an end to idleness by talking, not of love, as Dorus first suggests, but of Thirsil's departure from the abusive and unjust Chame. The storm that affords them this opportunity to converse bears little resemblance to the threatening twelve-day rage depicted by Sannazaro. Instead it recalls the "Westerne Wind [which] bloweth sore" in the September Eclogue of *The Shepheardes Calender*, causing Hobbinol and Diggon to sit "vnder the hill" that they may talk and tell their fill about ecclesiastical abuses. Like Myrtilus and Dorus, they "make a mocke at the blustring blast" by discoursing about far worse political storms.

As Myrtilus's story continues, we hear Thomalin's futile attempt to persuade Thirsil "with Chamus boyes to stay." We recognize in this plea not only Fletcher's own historical circumstance, but the circumstance of Colin Clout in the June Eclogue of the *Calender*,[11] where the poet records his own departure from "that paradise . . . whych Adam lost." Colin's pastoral companion, Hobbinol, describes "The simple ayre, the gentle warbling wynde / So calme, so coole, as no where else I fynde" where "systers nyne, which dwell on Parnasse hight, / Doe make them musick for their more delight" (4–5, 28–29). Echoing this familiar description of the *locus amoenus*, Thomalin exclaims to Thirsil:

> More sweet, or fruitfull streams where canst thou finde?
> Where fisher-lads, or Nymphs more fair, or kinde?
> The Muses' selves sit with the sliding Chame.
>
> (II.5.4–6)

Thirsil does not deny the pleasures of this world, but, like Colin Clout, makes it clear that they are pleasures undone by ill deed, and no longer available to him. As Rosalind refuses Colin's affections, so Chame treats Thirsil:

> Not I my Chame, but me proud Chame refuses:
> His froward spites my strong affections sever;
> Else, from his banks could I have parted never.
>
> (II.6.3–5)

Fletcher's loss of his academic position at the university finds expression in Thirsil's complaint of losing his net, his fish, and his boat:

> His stubborn hands my net hath broken quite:
> My fish (the guerdon of my toil and pain)
> He causelesse seaz'd, and with ungrateful spite
> Bestow'd upon a lesse deserving swain:
> The cost and labour mine, his all the gain.
>   My boat lies broke; my oares crackt, and gone.
>
> (II.7.1–6)

Thirsil's last remaining joy, like Colin's, is the consolation of song: "Nought h[as] he left me, but my pipe alone, / Which with his sadder notes may help his master moan" (II.7.7–8). Thirsil does not follow Colin's example so near as to smash his pipe, though the song his pipe moans becomes increasingly bitter, and even takes on a Theocritan flavor as he describes the treatment of Thelgon who went before him; for here Fletcher is recounting the injustice dealt to his father by Cambridge University. Chame had yielded Thelgon a costly boat and then "bequeath'd it to a wandring guest" (II.12.3). Then, after further arduous toils through winter time

> . . . Chame to Gripus gave it once again,
> Gripus the basest and most dung-hill swain,
> That ever drew a net, or fisht in fruitfull main.
>
> (II.14.6–8)

Thomalin's responses, "Ah Foolish Chame!" and "Ungrateful Chame!" echo Hobbinol's "Ah faithlesse Rosalind." Colin's beloved, like the ungrateful Chame, distributed her affection unjustly, and, even worse, scorned Colin's pipe. Yet, she does not diminish in beauty for being unfaithful; in fact, she is only desired the more by Colin for being less attainable. So too with Thirsil and the River

Cam. His leaving Chamus's shores only makes him long for them the more. Despite the injustice dealt him by the Chame, he knows the potential *otium* to be had in the fellowship he must leave behind:

> Thomalin, me thinks I heare thy speaking eye
> Woo me my posting journey to delay:
> But let thy love yeeld to necessitie:
> With thee, my friend, too gladly would I stay,
> And live, and die. . . .
>
> (II.20.1–5)

Thirsil resolves nonetheless to depart the Cam, and his departing speech contains, by way of loss, a familiar catalogue of pastoral ingredients as listed in Colin's "adieu delights" at the close of the *Calender*, and repeated by the uncouth swain in "Lycidas":

> Farewell ye streams, which once I loved deare;
> Farewell ye boyes, which on your Chame do float;
> Muses farewell, if there be Muses here;
> Farewell my nets, farewell my little boat:
> Come sadder pipe, farewell my merry note:
> My Thomalin, with thee all sweetnessed well;
> Think of thy Thirsil, Thirsil loves thee well.
> Thomalin, my dearest deare, my Thomalin, farewell.
>
> (II.24.1–8)

Here the poet, like his predecessors, preserves in symbolic images what he has lost. Colin's woods become streams; his flock is replaced by nets and boats, but the idyllic circumstance these things represent is essentially unchanged. The swain takes leave of the pleasant environs, the instruments of his vocation, and the company of his fellows. These final lines of his farewell also affirm that, as with Colin Clout and the uncouth swain in "Lycidas," Thirsil's deepest sorrow is the loss of the greatest pastoral joy: the intimacy of his fellow swain.

Like the eclogues of the *Calender*, each of Fletcher's seven eclogues has a particular problem that propels it. Fletcher's idyllic shores exist under less than ideal conditions, and the resulting academic and ecclesiastical conflicts he portrays serve as the source for pastoral rivalry. Just as Colin's rejection by Rosalind and his consequent rejecting of the pastoral delights link the *Calender*, so too Thirsil's complaints against, and consequent departure from, Chamus's shores connect the *Piscatorie Eclogues*. Just as Colin, hurt by Rosalind, directs his complaints at his shepherd's world, so too the complaints of Thirsil, rather than being directed toward a love from outside of the world, are aimed instead precisely at the supposedly blissful world of which he is a part.

The wide divergence between a recollected idyllic world and that world's actual miseries is something Fletcher handles in an interesting fashion by making a distinction between the unjust, authoritative "Chame" and the blissful "Chamus" world that Thirsil is sad to leave. Here again it is a case of Fletcher doing more overtly what his pastoral predecessors had done more subtly. This pastoral anomaly of an ideal world being governed by a real owner can be traced back to Virgil, where, in the first eclogue, we see Tityrus has the privilege of enjoying an idyllic life, turning "woodland musings on a delicate reed" and "lazing in the shade" (1.2,4), while his friend Meliboeus is forced to "flee" his "sweet fields, Abandon home" (1.3,4). Though Tityrus's world is clearly idyllic, the power who grants it to him, whom he calls "A God forever," is at best arbitrary, and at worst, unjust. For it is presumably this same power, the very "god," who exiles Meliboeus from his land.

Just as the land itself contains Tityrus's idyllic world, so too with Thirsil and the other swains in Fletcher's *Eclogues*. The Chamus shores and the fellowship enjoyed there make up the idyllic world, quite apart from the authority who governs those shores, giving or taking away boats in the same fashion as Virgil's remote landowner gives and takes away land. Thus, like the sweet fields of Virgil's first eclogue, the world of Fletcher's *Eclogues* is a world at once governed by, and at the same time independent of, administrative authority—in this case, the unjust Chame. This Chame does not belong to the world of Chamus any more than the authoritative elders of Cambridge University comprised the seventeenth-century world of Cambridge. They set the rules and determined the appointment of fellowships. However, the world of youthful rivalry and fellowship that we saw in chapter 2 is a world that thrives apart from, and often in spite of, such powers.

In Eclogue IV, Fletcher's river world, which in the first three eclogues has served as a parallel of the academic world, begins to parallel the ecclesiastical world as well. This additional meaning evolves rather naturally given Fletcher's waterfront setting and the familiar biblical piscatory linkage between fishermen and the disciples of Jesus.[12] In depicting his fishermen as fishers of men, Fletcher does not, however, abandon his academic allegory, but instead accomplishes what he does through a synthesis of meanings. Kastor asserts that "the social rather than religious aspects of pastoralism occupied the young Phineas Fletcher at Cambridge" (79), but in Eclogue IV it is not apparent that Fletcher ever made any clear distinction between the two. For here, "the particular lesson that he chooses to teach is determined by . . . [a] set of convictions and ideas" other than those of a purely academic world—"the role proper to a Christian minister" (Baldwin, "His Modern Readers," 470). In fact, for Phineas Fletcher there was no such thing as a purely academic world. Cambridge University, despite the new political entanglements wrought by the Reformation, retained its original and important function as a seminary for priests. As such, the study of pagan classics existed alongside theological and biblical study. One perhaps memorized as much poetry from classical myths as from the Bible.[13] Just so, in Spenser's or Fletcher's worlds, two worthy swains can debate about Christian discipleship in a world governed by the movements of Neptune, Flora, Phoebus, and Zephyr. Such a pagan and Christian synthesis was, of course, not only characteristic of Renaissance art, but necessary to Renaissance pastoral art. Fletcher's innovation was to include in that synthesis detailed descriptions of the academic world. Thus, in the *Eclogues*, the Arcadian pastoral world, the world of the academic poet, and the world of Christian discipleship all converge in the same poetry, something often credited to Milton's "Lycidas," written four years after Fletcher's *Eclogues* were printed at Cambridge.

As much as any of Fletcher's eclogues, Eclogue IV echoes *The Shepheardes Calender*, particularly the May Eclogue, while foreshadowing "Lycidas." It consists of a dialogue between Chromis and Thelgon (an indication that the *Eclogues* are not to be taken as a consecutive narrative, since Thelgon's death was lamented in Eclogue II). The eclogue opens with Thelgon's call to Chromis, which contains the familiar pastoral inquiry into a fellow swain's sadness: "Chromis my joy, why drop thy rainie eyes?" (1.1). Thelgon's first assumption regarding Chromis's sorrow demonstrates the ordering of pastoral priorities: "Seems that thy net is rent, and idle lies; / Thy merry pipe hangs broken on a bough" (1.3–4). Chromis's sadness is caused, he presumes, by some harm to his vocation as poet that has resulted in a lack of song.

When Chromis assures him that his "pipe is whole, and nets are new" (2.1), Thelgon makes the next most logical assumption, that his friend, lost to "loves new-kindled fire," is suffering from an unrequited love. In Chromis's case, however, a new twist is put upon the swain's conventional sorrow. Chromis's problem is not being loved too little, but just the opposite:

> But one I love, and he loves me again;
> In love this onely is my greatest sore,
> He loves so much, and I can love no more.
>
> (4.4–6)

At this point, the eclogue might still be a song in praise of a lover's devotion, but the next stanza makes it clear that romantic love is not the matter here:

> But when the fishers trade, once highly priz'd,
> And justly honour'd in those better times,
> By every lozel-groom I see despis'd;
> No marvel if I hate my jocond rimes,
> And hang my pipe upon a willow bough:
> Might I grieve ever, if I grieve not now.
>
> (5.1–6)

Conditioned by the previous eclogues, the reader here assumes that the eclogue has turned into yet another complaint against Chame, and that "the fishers trade" represents the scholar's profession and poet's prominence from which first Thelgon and then Thirsil have been banished. This assumption is, in part, true; for Chromis does hang up his pipe. We see in Thelgon's response to Chromis, however, that Chromis's real concern is not with the declining reputation of students and poets, but of Christian ministers. Theirs is "the fishers trade" that he sees "despis'd." Thelgon's reply thus clarifies as well the object of Chromis's inadequate love:

> Ah foolish boy! why should'st thou so lament
> To be like him, whom thou dost like so well?
> The Prince of fishers thousand tortures rent.
> To heav'n, lad, thou art bound: the way by hell.
>
> (6.1–4)

Chromis's love is a Christian love, but his human love is returned too abundantly by the divine Christ. In this inadequacy he resembles the "Prince of fishers," the apostle Peter,[14] who, after denying Christ, was embarrassed by Christ's asking three times, "Peter, do you love me?" Thus, not only in the suffering of which he complains, but in his failure to return to Christ's love, Chromis is "like him whom [he] dost like so well."

Thelgon's dismal assurance to Chromis (bound to heaven by way of hell) sets the tone for the elaborate criticisms of "the fishers trade" that Thelgon goes on to make. There have been in the past, he says, good fishers who "rule[d] their own boats, and use[d] their nets aright," (12.2), but "few were such, and now those few are gone" (12.6). He himself is among those departed, which is part of Chromis's lament: "no more our seas shall heare your melodie; / Your songs and shrilling pipes shall sound no more" (13.3–4). Thelgon's own description of those who have taken his place is filled with the familiar rivalry we have seen throughout: "Their floating boats with waves have leave to play, / Their rusty hooks all yeare keep holy-day" (14.5–6).

As Thelgon continues to criticize these fishers, the humor of his descriptions increases, but so too might the reader's confusion at the synthesis between the academic and the ecclesiastic taking place within those descriptions. For with the introduction of the "Prince of fishers" we began to read the "fishers trade" as an allegory for discipleship. In Thelgon's further descriptions, however, the depiction of university rivalry seems clearer than anywhere else in the eclogues. Since, as we have noted, Cambridge was in part a seminary, we can resolve that university and ecclesiastical rivalry are here mixed together:

> Some stretching in their boats supinely sleep,
> Seasons in vain recall'd, and windes neglecting:
> Others their hooks and baits in poison steep,
> Neptune himself with deathfull drugges infecting:
> . . . .
> Some teach to work, but have no hands to row:
> Some will be eyes, but have no light to see:
> Some will be guides, but have no feet to go:
> Some deaf, yet eares; some dumbe, yet tongues will be.
>
> (17.1–4; 18.1–4)

As the world of the student and the world of the minister converge, the "boats," which in Eclogue II were fellowships or academic positions, might here be regarded as parishes occupied by deficient ministers, unable to instruct or guide for lack of inspired vision or informed hearing.

In the following stanza in particular, we can visualize the material comfort and clerical arrogance of a stately bishop or a university rector:

> Some greater, scorning now their narrow boat,
> In mighty hulks and ships (like courts) do dwell;
> Slaving the skiffes that in their seas do float;
> Their silken sails with windes do proudly swell;
> Their narrow bottomes stretch they large and wide,
>   And make full room for luxurie and pride.
>
> (19.1–6)

The world that these failed fishers inhabit clearly takes us far beyond Chamus's shores. Thelgon tells us that "Where Tybers swelling waves his banks o'reflow, / There princely fishers dwell in courtly halls" (22.1–2). These "princely fishers" have forsaken the simplicity of the River Cam for a life replete with the riches and political trappings of the court. To establish himself at court was the goal of many a Cambridge student, a goal that meant leaving behind the pastoral joys of the university. Whether or not these fishers whom Thelgon condemns have made it to the court, they have, at least, given up their meager "boats" for something more lavish than an academic fellowship—namely, "hulks and ships (like courts)." Gone is the River Cam, and gone are the pastoral joys, the surest evidence of which is the lust for worldly wealth that has replaced the pastoral poverty of the simple fisher swain. These fishers, Thelgon says, "fish for steeples high with golden hooks" (22.6). With this loss of communality goes the joy of fellowship as well. The loss of these joys is the source of Chromis's lament. He hangs up his pipe for lack of simple and honest companions with whom to sing.

The final four stanzas of this eclogue are delivered by Algon, a pseudonym perhaps for Fletcher himself, who delivers a speech that makes sufficient answer to the conversation of Thelgon and Chromis. He directs their longing beyond their nostalgic look at Chamus's better days to the much earlier world of the Prince of Fishers, whom Milton will call the Pilot of the Galilean lake. Algon thus sings the praises of:

> Those fisher-swains, from whom our trade doth flow,
> That by the King of seas their skill were taught;

As they their boats on Jordan wave did row,
And catching fish, were by a Fisher caught;
    (Ah blessed chance! much better was the trade,
    That being fishers, thus were fishes made).

                                                    (28.1–6)

Fletcher here is getting full use of the language, enjoying the idea
that, as Simone Dorangeon points out, the original fishers of men
were themselves fishes caught by the Fisher-Christ. So while Chromis has spent the entire poem lamenting the "fishers trade,"
Algon quibbles his way into praising the "trade" (change of life)
that the apostles made from being fishermen to becoming fishes,
and then, once caught, fishers of men.

Algon tells the discouraged Chromis that he should seek to please
the King of the seas. "Let not thy net, thy hook, thy singing cease,"
he urges him, "And pray these tempests may be turn'd to peace"
(30.5–6). In this, and in his parting prayer with which the eclogue
ends, Algon is holding up the possibility of *otium*. As Christ calmed
the waters for the frantic apostles, so Argon prays: "Chide thou the
windes, and furious waves allay" (31.4). The relief from such a
storm would be a calm that would then be celebrated in the fellowship of song, songs in praise of the king of Christian *otium*: "So on
thy shore the fisher-boys shall sing. / Sweet songs of peace to our
sweet peaces King" (31.6–7).

Earlier I made a case for Thomalin and Thirsil exhibiting, even
more clearly than Colin and Hobbinol, the platonic love of which
pastoral *otium* is born. Thomalin, unable to enjoy the *otium* of fel-
lowhip because of a captured heart, is instructed by Thirsil of a
higher love: "I love with sweeter love, and more delight: / But most
I love that love, which to my love h[as] right" (25.8–9). The
sweeter love is of a divine nature, and is reserved not for lovers but
for pastoral companions. This lesson is illustrated in a decidedly
collegiate fashion in Eclogue VII ("The Prize"), the last of the *Piscatorie Eclogues*. Though most of it is taken up with two swains'
praise for their beloveds, the eclogue is more aptly read as a celebration of the pastoral fellowship that brings together rival shepherds and fisher-boyes in mutual daylong frolic. More than any of
the other eclogues in this collection or in Spenser's *Calender*, this
eclogue illustrates the joys of youthful rivalry and fellowship upon
which the pastoral world depends.

Unlike the other six eclogues, which are narrated in the third person, Eclogue VII opens in the first person, with a narrator who is clearly a part of the action:

> The morn saluting, up I quickly rise,
> And to the green I poste; for on this day
> Shepherd and fisher-boyes had set a prize,
> Upon the shore to meet in gentle fray.
>
> (2.1–4)

The "gentle fray" consists primarily of a singing contest between Thomalin, representing the best of the fisher-boyes, and his rival Daphnis, the sweetest singer among the shepherds. The contest begins with the spirited arrival of these two singers in company with their fellow swains.

As our narrator arrives at "the green," we are first witness to the procession of the shepherds to the appointed spot. Here Fletcher provides a memorable pastoral scene of frolic, youth, and song in which even the animals are enraptured to the point of forgetfulness:

> There soon I view the merry shepherd-swains
> March three by three, clad all in youthful green:
> And while the sad recorder sweetly plains,
> Three lovely Nymphs (each several now between,
> More lovely Nymphs could no where els be seen,
> Whose faces snow their snowy garments stains)
> With sweeter voices sit their pleasing strains.
>   Their flocks flock round about; the horned rammes,
>   And ewes go silent by, while wanton lambes
> Dancing along the plains, forget their milky dammes.
>
> (3.1–11)

Such a scene is a familiar one to any reader of pastoral literature. We can envision the nymphs and understand the meaning implied by the shepherds "clad all in youthful green." Far less familiar is the piscatorial parade that follows:

> Scarce were the shepherds set, but straight in sight
> The fisher-boyes came driving up the stream;
> Themselves in blue, and twenty sea-nymphs bright
> In curious robes, that well the waves might seem:
> All dark below, the top like frothy cream:
> Their boats and masts with flowres, and garlands dight;
> And round the swannes guard them with armies white:

Their skiffes by couples dance to sweetest sounds,
Which running cornets breath to full plain grounds,
That strikes the rivers face, and thence more sweet rebounds.

(4.1–11)

The blue dress of the Chamus's fisher-boyes and the "curious robes" of their surrounding nymphs come wrought with some mystery—mystery bred by, if nothing else, simple unfamiliarity. The shepherds are quite literally down to earth. That which comes from the water is never quite so simple. Fletcher, nevertheless, brings the two rival groups together in one common setting for a day of friendly rivalry.

This festival of rival swains bears unmistakable resemblance to the collegiate rivalries, both within and outside of the university. One specific parallel clearly connects this eclogue with the historical context from which it arises. Thirsil, the bearer of Fletcher's piscatory pseudonym, is qualified to judge the contest between Thomalin and Daphnis because of his close connection with both groups. Phineas Fletcher, we know, after leaving Cambridge, went to Derbyshire and became a country pastor; as it is described in the eclogue:

Thirsil their judge, who now's a shepherd base,
But late a fisher-swain, till envious Chame
Had rent his nets, and sunk his boats with shame;
So robb'd the boyes of him, and him of all his game.

(5.9–11)

These lines bring us back to Eclogue II, and remind us again that the historical world in which Fletcher lived and the piscatory world that he created, while not one and the same, are often close enough so as to be distinguished from one another only by such details as names and nets. For, "shepherd or fisher I am still the same," wrote Fletcher in *Sicelides*, a piscatory drama performed at Trinity College, "I am a sea guest not for gaine, but game."

In keeping with both pastoral and academic rules, the love objects of whom Daphnis and Thomalin sing are both from outside this present pastoral world of fellowship. Neither Daphnis's Phoebus nor Thomalin's Stella was discovered during these swains' common observance of their respective vocations of shepherding and fishing. Daphnis tells us of his immediate love for Phoebus, whom he found not while pastoring sheep but during the more violent activity of hunting.

> First her I saw, when tir'd with hunting toyl
> In shady grove spent with the weary chace,
> Her naked breast lay open to the spoil.
>
> (10.1–3)

Daphnis's hunting, of course, yields him a catch to tantalize, if not appease, his youthful hunger. Thomalin finds love's joy and sorrow in a similarly appropriate act of the appetite, while feasting:

> At Proteus feast, where many a goodly boy,
> And many a lovely lasse did lately meet;
> There first I found, there first I lost my joy.
>
> (15.1–3)

Like Colin's Rosalind, Phoebus and Stella are but the objects of song; singing itself is the concern of this eclogue, a fact that becomes clear as the amoebean nears its finish. We discover that the contest was no contest at all, but an occasion for exchanging songs. Rather than concluding in a battle over the "Prize," which the eclogue's title might lead us to expect, the two swains share an exchange of gifts and compliments, each lavishing upon the other a special treasure that he has been given for his own singing. Thus it is that pastoral rivalry turns naturally to fellowship.

Before leaving off their singing, the singers engage in a final boasting match in which they call attention to the dangers of one another's vocation and praise the pleasures of their own:

> *Daphnis.* Thrice happy swains! thrice happy shepherds fate!
> *Thomalin.* Ah blessed life! ah blessed fishers state!
> Your pipes asswage your love; your nets maintain you.
> *Daphnis.* Your lambkins clothe you warm; your flocks sustain you.
> You fear no stormie seas, nor tempests roaring.
> *Thomalin.* You sit not rots or burning starres deploring:
> In calms you fish; in roughs use songs and dances.
> *Daphnis.* More do you fear your Loves sweet-bitter glances,
> Then certain fate, or fortune ever changing.
> *Thomalin.* Ah that the life in seas so safely ranging,
> Should with loves weeping eye be sunk, and drowned!
>
> (32.1–11)

This exchange, which serves to catalogue briefly the common joys of pastoral poverty and simplicity, subsides, like the praises of Phoebus and Stella, into an exchange of complimentary gifts: "Thou gentle boy, what prize may well reward thee?" Daphnis asks his rival. Thomalin's reply is just as gracious: "Thine be the prize: may Pan and Phoebus grace thee." The "prize" or praise is given and declined by each of them "Since," as Thirsil puts it, "none of both deserve, when both so well deserve it" (35.11). Such humility characterizes the joy of "poverty" to which these swains are accustomed, and which, by their humble spirit, they represent. They stand in contrast to the proud fishers of Eclogue IV, and the dunghill Gripus and disdainful Chame of Eclogue II.

It is as though Fletcher goes out of his way to bring his *Eclogues* to a close not with the bitterness that fills so many of his other complaints, but with the spirit of pastoral joy that makes Chamus's shores so difficult to leave. He had to depart those shores, nevertheless, and, as Thirsil, the fisher turned pastor of a flock, he brings that former world to himself by inviting the rival fisher and shepherd swains to a feast that is in keeping with his station and suitable to their simplicity:

> Vouchsafe with me to take some short refection:
> Excesse, or daint my lowly roofs maintain not;
> Pears, apples, plummes, no sugred made confection.
>
> (37.2–4)

Fletcher goes to extremes in this final eclogue to exhibit the power of the divine love that Thirsil had earlier described to Thomalin. Rivalry is so supplanted by fellowship at this gathering that even quarreling over nymphs is set aside:

> So up they rose, and by Love's sweet direction
> Sea-nymphs with shepherds sort: sea-boyes complain not
> That wood-nymphs with like love them entertain not.
>
> (37.5–7)

Whether by neglect or intention, the narrator, our guide into this *locus amoenus*, vanishes. The final lines of the eclogue are delivered in the third person rather than in the more intimate first person with which the eclogue began. Our last look at Fletcher's world of Chamus's shores is a sad but serene one. We leave shepherds and fisher-boyes enjoying harmony, characterized naturally enough by songs that propel the day forward: "And all the day to songs and dances lending, / Too swift it runnes, and spends too fast in spending" (37.8–9). The eclogue concludes, quite appropriately, with a sense of joy, had and then lost. Such were Fletcher's experiences at Cambridge University. He was a poet who knew all about endings and could appreciate, even if his readers could not, the full significance of the final line of his *Eclogues*: "With day their sports began, with day they take their ending."

Fletcher's closing eclogue would not be the last poem in which a familiar swain would surrender his speaking role to the impersonal voice of an anonymous narrator. In fact, another loss-inspired Cambridge pastoral would appear in print four years after the publication of Fletcher's *Piscatorie Eclogues*. That few readers come to John Milton's "Lycidas" having first read the *Piscatorie Eclogues* would not likely have surprised Fletcher, who, already forty-nine years old when his works were finally published at Cambridge, regarded his pastoral and epic endeavors alike as the products of his youth. Responding to the affectionate manner in which Edward Belowes prefaced his collected works, Fletcher wrote in the dedication:

> such is the eye whereby you have viewed these raw Essayes of my very unripe yeares, and almost childhood. How unseasonable are Blossomes in Autumne! (unless perhaps in this age, where are more flowers then fruit). I am entering my Winter, and yet these Blossoms of my first Spring must now shew themselves to our ripe wits, which certainly will give them no other entertainment but derision.

At least one ripe Cambridge wit gave Fletcher's works serious attention rather than derision. Milton's lament for a drowned classmate becomes, among other things, a pastoral recollection of his academic days—not on the banks of the Cam, but on its "high lawns"—and the occasion for a reproof of unworthy Christian pastors. The uncouth swain of "Lycidas" is, in his blue mantle, especially familiar to readers of the *Eclogues* and *The Shepheardes Calender*, who recognize in his song a nostalgic sense of loss, not just for a deceased friend but for "*the delights of youth generally*," that is, the loss of the pastoral world.

6

"The Uncouth Swain"

WILLING TO SEE JOHN MILTON IN THE VERY MANNER IN WHICH HE fashioned himself—as a direct descendent of Virgil—many critics have acclaimed his assimilation of the Christian with the classical, while greatly underestimating his more immediate reliance upon his English ancestry. These claims often originate with Milton's pastoral debut in "Lycidas," which is described by Joseph Wittreich as having, in its ascent toward prophesy, vaulted beyond the limits of tradition, transcending and transforming pastoral: "Forms within forms, visions within visions, each meditating the other—orbs within orbs, cycles and epicycles—*Lycidas* achieves what has recently been credited to Coleridge: the extension of pastoral to its outward bound, which is prophesy" (65). The extension of pastoral to its outward bound of prophesy, of course, can be found as early as Virgil's Eclogue IV. Much of the originality accredited to Milton, I find, comes from critics who see him as the great predecessor of the romantic poets, rather than as a descendent of Renaissance poets. Viewed as a harbinger of nineteenth-century poetic thought, Milton appears radically innovative. Seen as an inheritor of sixteenth-century and seventeenth-century poetic thought, Milton may be seen, without diminishing his poetic achievement, as suitably conventional. The achievement in "Lycidas" lies not in its looking ahead so much as in its looking backward: in the poet's assimilation of, and response to, his pastoral predecessors, who, in the case of Spenser and Fletcher, were also his Cambridge predecessors.[1] My aim in this final chapter is to reassert "Lycidas" as a conventional English pastoral while exploring—in light of *The Shepheardes Calender* and the *Piscatorie Eclogues*—precisely what those three terms mean together.

Samuel Johnson's famous charge of insincerity against "Lycidas" is responsible for misdirecting many readers away from the poem and toward John Milton's actual feelings for Edward King, for Cambridge, and for John Milton—toward, in other words, that which is essentially unknowable. Not that the questions are not interesting ones: How well did Milton know King? Was Milton stirred by King's death toward an idyllic reminiscence of his days at Cambridge, which elsewhere he speaks of with indifference? What is the distance between the "machinery of the poem and the feelings it purports to express?"[2] Is it insincere artistry or genuine personal grief that prompts Milton to write "But O the heavy change now thou art gone"?

"Passion plucks no berries from the myrtle and ivy," claims Dr. Johnson, "nor calls upon Arethuse and Mincius, nor tells of 'rough satyrs and fauns with cloven heels. Where there is leisure for fiction, there is little grief" (*Lives*, 163). The implications of such a statement are vast—permitting, nay requiring, one to discount any genuine emotional presence in any number of literary works before and after Milton. As many critics have pointed out, Johnson's own preoccupation with the poem's use of conventions disregards a powerful emotional presence in the poem that many since have likewise ignored. In the words of Barbara Johnson: "these approaches focus exclusively on generic considerations; they do not speak directly to the question of how such a convention-bound poem can speak with such power" (69). Perceiving the pastoral conventions as an indication of the poem's lack of emotion, critics in the line of Samuel Johnson ignore the possibility that deep grief might, in fact, prompt fiction, that such passion may do little else but pluck berries.

Louis Kampf goes so far as to call Milton's use of pastoral "a foolish irrelevance" since the pastoral tradition "will hardly lead to reflections on the meaning of death,"[3] an assertion that demonstrates a misunderstanding not just of "Lycidas" but of the pastoral tradition itself, which begins with a reflection on the meaning of death in the very first idyll of Theocritus, when Thyrsis sings "The Affliction of Daphnis." The song begins by asking: "Where were ye, Nymphs, when Daphnis pined?" (I.2). Such questions and such songs become part of pastoral convention, and Milton's nearly identical repetition of Theocritus's line in "Lycidas"—"Where were ye Nymphs when the remorselesse deep . . ."—while obviously conventional, is just as obviously part of a thorough pastoral contemplation of the meaning of death.

So fundamental are the generic pastoral aspects of the poem to

Hamilton that he sees Milton's own age figuring into his choice of
the pastoral mode. "That Edward King drowned in 1637 was an
accident," he says, "but it need not have been an accident that Milton, who was 29 in that year, decided to write a pastoral elegy on
his death" ("Grene Path," 4). Both Virgil and Spenser, Hamilton
notes, were twenty-nine (give or take two years in Spenser's case)[4]
when they completed their pastoral works. Hamilton's implication
is that Milton, in writing "Lycidas," was strictly imitating the pastoral precedent set before him—doing, as it were, what his literary
ancestry would have him do.

At the other extreme of those who see Milton's preoccupation in
writing "Lycidas" as chiefly or solely literary are those who not
only find deep feeling reflected in the poem, but presume to know
just what that deep feeling is. Martin Evans, for example, in his
book *The Road from Horton: Looking Backwards in "Lycidas,"* offers a psychological explanation for the poem's creation that coin-
cides with Hamilton's artistic one. Evans sees Milton in "Lycidas"
(as Hamilton sees Spenser in *The Shepheardes Calender*) moving
from pastoral recluse to active poet. He notes that the "drastic
change [from Horton to Europe] suggests that Milton underwent
what Daniel J. Levinston has called an Age Thirty Transition, a period of psychological crisis in which one's past is reappraised and
one's future redefined" (7).

Assertions that "Lycidas" is the product of either artistic or psychological anxiety or even of Milton's actual grief do not bring us
much nearer to the poem. Neither, unfortunately, does an attempt
to know the poet's feelings toward the selfsame hill upon which he
and Lycidas were nursed. Milton's career at Cambridge, while not
as lengthy as Phineas Fletcher's, bears some resemblance to his
predecessor's, whose *Piscatorie Eclogues* recorded the turbulence
of academic politics on the banks of the River Cam. The young
John Milton soon became acquainted with that turbulence. His conflict with his tutor, Chappell, and the subsequent intervention of the
Cambridge authorities are well known. The cry "Ungrateful
Chame" echoes Fletcher's disappointment at the mistreatment of
his father and himself. Milton, at least initially, seems not even to
have enjoyed at Cambridge the fondness from which such disappointment springs. "The little girl of Christ's"[5] writes to Diodati
from London in the first of his Latin elegies: "At present I feel no
concern about returning to the sedgy Cam and am troubled by no
nostalgia for my forbidden quarters there. The bare fields, so nig-

gardly of pleasant shade, have no charm for me. How wretchedly suited that place is to the worshipers of Phoebus! It is disgusting to be constantly subjected to the threats of a rough tutor and to other indignities which my spirit cannot endure."[6] Were they "bare fields" then in which the poet and Lycidas drove their flocks "ere the high lawns appear'd / Under the glimmering eyelids of the morn"?[7] Here in the above passage perhaps are the grumblings found in the letters of any college freshman, then or now. However, we do little better by trying to match Milton's later feelings toward his university with the fond remembrance spoken by the swain in "Lycidas."

Four years after completing "Lycidas," in 1642, Milton wrote in a pamphlet that he regarded the suburb in London where he then dwelt to be a more honorable place than Cambridge University, "Which, as in the time of her better health and mine own younger judgment, I never greatly admired, so now much less".[8] What we see here, and elsewhere in Milton, is a general dissatisfaction with the university system. "While at Cambridge," Masson tells us, "Milton was one of those younger spirits,—Ramists, Baconians, Platonists, as they might be called, collectively or distributively,— who were at war with the methods of the place, and did not conceal their hostility" (272). Later in life, Milton would advocate "a radical reform of the system of the English Universities" (272). More immediately, his dissatisfaction would prompt others to rumor that he had departed from his university on bad terms, a claim Milton refuted. It may be then that, like Fletcher, Milton loved "Chamus" and the "Chamus Boys" but despised the unjust Chame. To search beyond "Lycidas" for a hint of such fondness, however, yields little.

In the same pamphlet in which Milton voices his preference for his London suburb, he speaks of the respect accorded him by the fellows at Cambridge. He uses the occasion of the pamphlet "to acknowledge publicly, with all grateful mind, that more than ordinary respect which I found, above any of my equals, at the hands of those courteous and learned men, the Fellows of that College wherein I spent some years; who at my parting . . . signified many ways how much better it would content them that I would stay."[9] His description here is of the fellows' love for him, and of their regret, not his. Ten years later, in another statement about his departure from Cambridge, it is again the loss of the fellows, not his own loss, that he acknowledges: "I . . . of my own accord went home, leaving even a sense of my loss among most of the Fellows of my College, by whom I had in no ordinary degree been regarded"[10] Again, of Milton's own loss we hear nothing, making the heavy loss of "Lycidas" increasingly suspect.

By all reports, Horton, where Milton retreated to live after graduation, was by far a more idyllic world than Cambridge University. "Now was the time for the youth to take in those 'images of rural nature,' " says Masson of Milton's life at Horton. Masson's description of the rural beauty at Horton is more idyllic, perhaps, than even Milton himself could imagine.[11] Here Milton's "youthful idealism" combined with his "ideal surroundings," and he created "L'Allegro" and "Il Penseroso." Cory refers to these days as Milton's "fullest days of detachment and dreams" ("The School," 352). Such days sound almost pastoral, until we recall that the central pastoral joy requires that the swain be just the opposite of detached. Engagement in a circle of fellow swains, intimacy and friendship: these are the ingredients of the pastoral joy of fellowship that Milton, detached and dreamy, did not enjoy at Horton as, perhaps, he had at Cambridge. King's death would be a sorrowful reminder of this fact, an occasion for recalling the life of learned friendships that he had had, and chose to leave behind—and now, in the case of Edward King, had lost tragically and permanently. Not that Milton's life and relationships at Cambridge were at all idyllic, for we certainly know otherwise, but that remembrance might, at least in poetry, make them so. Again, however, only in "Lycidas" do we have any record of such feelings of loss.

A stubborn attempt to prove Dr. Johnson wrong by finding out precisely what Milton really felt, therefore, leaves one deservedly no nearer the meaning of "Lycidas" than Johnson himself. If we wish to counter the claim that "Lycidas" is but a masterfully wrought literary exercise, we need to seek within the poem itself the source of the emotions of grief, sorrow, and nostalgia. How, then, can such a convention-bound poem speak with such power? Fittingly, the poem's emotional power resides, not separately from the poem's conventional pastoral ingredients, but within them. For it was not "Lycidas" Samuel Johnson misunderstood, but pastoral itself, regarding it as an exhaustible formula.[12] Pastoral is not about berries, ivy, satyrs, or fauns, but the ideas and emotions that these conventional images embody. When we understand the significance of such conventions as they have come down to Milton from Theocritus and Virgil and more immediately from Spenser and Fletcher, we see that they are conventions charged with emotional content stemming from the experience and subsequent loss of joys that might be framed into a particular time and place. As in the case of his two English predecessors, the time in "Lycidas" is youth, and the place is the recollected collegiate world of Cambridge that Milton and King inhabited "both together." The emotional power of "Lycidas" results from the compression into one hundred and ninety-three lines of blank verse of the emotionally charged pastoral themes, images, and ideas developed in the works of Spenser and Fletcher.

Interestingly, of all the poems preceding "Lycidas" in *Justa Edovardo King*, the Cambridge volume memorializing King, Milton's is the first to offer a pastoral response. Milton seems to have understood that pastoral—more than any other poetic genre—is born of and responds to loss. As Alpers observes, separation and loss are what give the speaker in "Lycidas" his voice ("Modern Criticism," 472). Anthony Varney suggests that the very word "uncouth" used to describe the swain in the poem's final lines can be read to mean lonely and forsaken, rather than simply rustic.[13] After all his singing, Milton's swain remains lonely and forsaken at Lycidas's death. "The author," the headnote tells us, "bewails a learned friend." Like Fletcher's Thyrsil, Spenser's Colin, Virgil's Meliboeus, and Theocritus's Thyrsis before him, the singer grieves the loss of fellowship. Asking the muse to bless his "destin'd Urn," the poet works, like those before him, ekphrastically, seeking to preserve with song what has been lost. Immediately following his request to the muse comes a fourteen-line passage describing the idyllic world he formerly shared with Lycidas. The companionship of the two shepherds comprises every line, "Together both" being inverted two lines later into "both together." As Hobbinol's memorable description of the *locus amoenus* in the *Calender*'s June Eclogue serves to highlight Colin's solitude in the January and December Eclogues, just so this shepherd's brief reminiscence of him and his companion sharing a common place, flock, and song serves to emphasize his utter solitude in the rest of the poem: "Now thou art gone, and never must return."

"It is because that world and time once had meaning as defined through the person of Lycidas," says Robert Bourdette, "that the mind of the speaker keeps coming back to versions of that ideal pastoral world for an answer" (15). That the mind of the singer returns to a world of pastoral joys in the above passage is clear, but that he returns looking for answers is certainly not. The speaker proposes no more than pastoral itself promises, "to bewail a learned friend." The framing of his reminiscence in pastoral stasis encourages that grief. If others would look for answers in "Lycidas," the singer himself seems to understand that his pastoral poem cannot provide them. The questions with which he comes armed are but the rhetorical kind. "Where were ye nymphs?" he asks, and then answers himself six lines later with another rhetorical question: "Had ye been there—for what could that have done?" The swains's only real question, "What boots it with uncessant care / To tend the homely slighted shepherd's trade?" is answered by Phoebus's conventional pastoral reply regarding fame. The other gods, rather than offering answers, only ask the obvious: "What hard mishap hath doom'd this gentle swain?" or "Who hath reft . . . my dearest pledge?"

As Colin discovers in *The Shepheardes Calender*, pastoral does not provide intellectual or theological solutions to the problem of loss. His pastoral companion, Hobbinol cannot explain Rosalind's unfaithfulness; he can but provide the consolation of song. And song is what comprises "Lycidas." Alpers, calling himself a literalist, notes that the purpose of "Lycidas" "is not to solve a problem or console the speaker or dramatize a situation but to 'sing for Lycidas'—that is, properly commemorate the dead shepherd" ("Modern Criticism," 479). Such song, Alpers would admit, does provide some consolation, but as I have argued earlier, we cannot ask of pastoral what it does not promise to deliver. Pastoral does not bring Daphnis back to life, spare Meliboeus his loss of land, heal Colin of his love melancholy, or restore Thirsil to the River Cam, nor does it take away the singer's grief in "Lycidas" by providing answers. The look backward is precisely that. The singer's mind returns to a former time and place, not for answers, but to see again that time and place; the singer's idyllic re-creation of this time and place in song serves its own end. The grief in "Lycidas" may well be actual, the nostalgia, perhaps, accidental. Perhaps Milton, even at the magic age of twenty-nine, did not yet realize that nostalgia comes, as it were, with the pastoral territory.

Part of the achievement of "Lycidas" lies in the problem the poet confronts. The loss of Milton's uncouth swain is more complete and more complicated than that of his pastoral predecessors. He mourns not just a deceased friend, but a drowned and irrecoverable corpse. His response to this double loss is nonetheless a properly pastoral—that is, ekphrastic, one. He offers not a simple Christian solution, but, like Colin in the November Eclogue of the *Calender*, the Christian hope of resurrection intermingled with pastoral imagery. As pastoral served to re-create an idyllic image of the "high lawns" of the past, so it now furnishes an image of Lycidas's redemption:

> Weep no more, wofull Shepherds, weep no more;
> For Lycidas your sorrow is not dead,
> Sunk though he be beneath the watry floore:
> So sinks the day-starre in the Ocean bed,
> And yet anon repairs his drooping head,
> And tricks his beams, and with new spangled ore,
> Flames in the forehead of the morning skie:
> So Lycidas sunk low, but mounted high
> Through the dear might of him that walk'd the waves;
> Where other groves, and other streams along,
> With Nectar pure his oazie locks he laves,
> And heares the unexpressive nuptiall song;
> There entertain him all the Saints above
> In solemn troups and sweet societies,
> That sing, and singing in their glory move,
> And wipe the tears forever from his eye.
>
> (165–81)

No heavenly Jerusalem here. Satyrs and cloven-heeled fauns are all that is lacking in what must surely be one of the most classically pagan descriptions of the Kingdom of God ever depicted. The singer's heavenly pastoral grove and its accompanying entertainment replace the imageless loss of Lycidas's drowned body just as his earlier description of "the self-same hill" replaced the irrecoverable loss of the poet's past.

"Lycidas" furnishes a conventionally pastoral response to loss that clearly demonstrates the emotional range of those conventions. It remains to consider the particularly English and academic qualities of the pastoral ingredients with which Milton constructs his poem. His choice of an English pastoral to commemorate his dead friend is entirely suitable. This choice also explains, I believe, why, conscious of his predecessors in this genre, Milton chose to provide a pastoralization of Cambridge and a re-creation of Edward King as an ideal shepherd when, as we have seen, no particular fondness for either is exhibited beyond this poem.

Noting that "pastoral convention" is not disconnected from the "individual and the personal," Alpers explains why and in what manner passion plucks berries:

> Virgil's shepherds come together to entertain each other, in friendship and in friendly rivalry. Seen in this light, pastoral conventions are not fixed procedures imposed by impersonal tradition, but are the usages of other poets—a community of past singers, analogous to the community of young Cambridge poets who wrote and collected memorial verses for Edward King. Poetic convention in this sense—the shared practice of those who come together to sing—can enable individual expression, because the poet is seen as responsive to, even when challenging, his predecessors and fellows. It is this process that is constitutive of poet and poem in "Lycidas." ("Modern Criticism," 470)

Real and individual emotion may well find a place within tradition, which, as Alpers says, is not impersonal but communal. Giving one's voice to pastoral song means connecting oneself to a community of singers. Alpers finds an analogue to Virgil's shepherds in the Cambridge poets whose works, along with Milton's "Lycidas," comprised *Justa Edovardo King*. This seems plausible, at least rhetorically, since the uncouth swain in "Lycidas" shares a common grief with the other singers in the collection of commemorative verse. On the other hand, Milton's poem is distinguished from the others. A clearly superior poem to those that come before it, it comes last in the volume, as in a procession of orators, and is far more encompassing in theme and content than those that precede it. As the only English pastoral, it attempts successfully to place itself in a different "community of past singers." In effect, the poem might be said, conscious of its mediocre surroundings, to successfully canonize itself. With generous "usages of other poets," Milton's poem takes its place in the line of his two Cambridge predecessors in pastoral, Spenser and Fletcher, who, in Virgilian fashion, both went on to write lengthy epics.

Milton's poem, furthermore, is the only one that records, not just the speaker's loss of King, but his loss of Cambridge as well. Placing himself in the community of the English pastoralists who preceded him at Cambridge and recorded the departure from "the delights of youth generally," Milton seems to have recognized that the recollection and depiction of collegiate land- and mindscapes was a convention that now belonged to English pastoral. It is necessary, in making this case, to see more specifically the "usages" Milton made of his predecessors in creating "Lycidas."

"By 1627," Cory tells us, "the names of Giles and Phineas Fletcher must have been prominent at Milton's own university, Cambridge, where he was a novitiate in poetry for seven years" ("Spenser," 313). The "School of the Fletchers," in fact, enjoyed a good deal more notoriety at Cambridge than is generally accredited to them. This group of professed Spenserians was Milton's most direct link to Spenser, the Cambridge master of English pastoral verse.[14] To one unfamiliar with Fletcher's *Eclogues*, "Lycidas" appears far more radically original than is actually the case. Just as Fletcher avoided duplication of Spenser's *Calender* by creating a piscatory world, Milton's choice of traditional pastoral for "Lycidas" allowed him to describe the drowning of a former classmate while avoiding any obvious repetition of Fletcher's shore world. "Lycidas" nonetheless contains several specific echoes of Fletcher's *Piscatorie Eclogues*, and Fletcher's work, filled with water imagery and fond remembrances of Cambridge, served as a perfect bridge from Spenser's *Calender* to Milton's elegiac song.

Like the initially anonymous and solitary figure in *The Shepheardes Calender*—"A Shepheards boye (no better doe him call)"—the uncouth swain of "Lycidas" comes forward and speaks alone. After his avowal to not let Lycidas "flote upon his watry biere / Unwept, and welter to the parching wind / Without the meed of some melodious tear" (12–14), the speaker calls upon the sisters of the sacred well to "somewhat loudly sweep the string" to summon a gentle muse to help him with his song. Following this invocation, as I noted above, the speaker turns immediately to a nostalgic recollection of an idyllic world of timeless *otium* "by fountain, shade, and rill" that he and Lycidas inhabited without regard for time, driving afield at daybreak and staying until the evening star made its descent. This "self-same hill" described through the eyes of loss recalls not just the fields that Meliboeus leaves to Tityrus, but that "paradise" that Colin leaves to Hobbinol: "Heare wander may thy flock early or late, / Withouten dreade of Wolves to bene ytost / The lovely layes here mayst thou freely boste" and the happy shores of Chamus that Thirsil leaves behind: "More sweet, or fruitfull streams where canst thou finde? / Where fisherlads, or Nymphs more fair, or kinde? / The Muses selves sit with the sliding Chame."

Here in his most immediate pastoral predecessor, of course, Milton finds his own university turned into piscatory bliss. Turning the sliding Chame back into fountains, shades, and rills, Milton accomplishes more subtly a re-creation of the academic into pastoral remembrance. Yet, his speaker recognizes and voices even more dramatically than his predecessors that this perfect place he describes depended solely upon the companionship he shared with Lycidas. Loss of that friendship meant loss of *otium*, and in "Lycidas" even the landscape knows it—his loss being likened, among other things, to "Taintworm to the weanling Herds."

When the shepherd goes on to voice the familiar cry against his trade, "Alas! what boots it with uncessant care / To tend the homely slighted Shepherd's trade, / And strictly meditate the thanklesse Muse?" (64–66), we recall Piers's complaint in the October Eclogue of the *Calender*, but are returned even more immediately to Fletcher's fourth eclogue, where Chromis complains: "Ah wretched fishers! born to hate and strife; / To others good, but to your rape and spoil. / This is the briefest summe of fishers life" (IV.10.1–3). Milton's singer seeks fame from his labor in poetry, and wonders if it is not better, like others, "To sport with Amaryllis in the shade, / Or with the tangles of Neaera's hair?" (68–69). Chromis desires some honor for his piety, and watches instead "foolish lads, that think with waves to play" (16.1). Both men, in effect, desire an audience for what they know to be good, and both of them are met with careless indifference. Not surprisingly, they both receive the same reply to their lament.

Milton's singer is interrupted by Phoebus, who tells him:

> Fame is no plant that growes on mortall soil,
> Nor in the glistring foil
> Set off to th' world, nor in broad rumour lies,
> But lives and spreads aloft by those pure eyes
> And perfect witnesse of all-judging Jove.

(1.78–82)

Fame, as Phoebus explains to the slighted shepherd, is an eternal gift, eternally granted. It is, in other words, a reward like the salvation granted to the scorned fishers. As Algon tells Chromis:

> Those fisher-swains, from whom our trade doth flow,
> That by the King of seas their skill were taught;
> . . . .
> Those happy swains, in outward shew unblest,

Were scourg'd, were scorn'd, yet was this losse their gain:

. . . .

For that short wo in this base earthly dwelling,
Enjoying joy all excellence excelling.

(28.1–2; 29.1–2, 5–6)

These passages not only forecast Phoebus's reply but look as well to the descriptions of Lycidas's resurrection "Through the dear might of him that walk'd the waves . . . In the blest Kingdoms meek of joy and love" (l.173, 177).

The waves and nymphs and accompanying water images that belong to Fletcher's piscatory world Milton finds suitable to his poem. As he contemplates his friend's drowning, his green world becomes more and more a blue one. The arrival in a procession of river gods of "Camus, reverend Sire" lamenting the loss of his "dearest pledge" is conventional enough, perhaps, so as not to connect "Lycidas" directly with Fletcher's *Eclogues*. The one who follows Camus in Milton's procession, however, explicitly links the two poems.

The pilot of the Galilean Lake shows up first, recall, in Fletcher's Eclogue IV as the "Prince of fishers," and there, as in "Lycidas," his appearance is the occasion for a resounding denunciation of the clergy. Fletcher's piscatory world, with its references to the "first swains" who "their boats on Jordan's wave did row," is much better suited to the fisherman-saint who in "Lycidas" speaks inappropriately as an authority on shepherding. The Pilot's famed attack on clergy in "Lycidas," while it can be traced to Spenser's *Calender*,[15] comes largely from Fletcher, where Thelgon and Chromis together deliver a seventeen-stanza attack on unlearned, wealthy, and slothful clergy that goes far beyond the reprimand of Cuddie or the Pilot of the Galilean Lake:

> Some teach to work, but have no hands to row:
> Some will be eyes, but have no light to see:
> Some will be guides, but have no feet to go:
> Some deaf, yet eares; some dumbe, yet tongues will be:
> Dumb, deaf, lame, blinde, and maim'd; yet fishers all:
> Fit for no use, but store an hospital.

(18.1–6)

What Fletcher catalogues in a stanza, Milton achieves with the weight of two words: "*Blind mouthes!*" The impossibility of the two words together is jolting, but as the line continues, we recognize its conventionality, seeing Fletcher's piscatory complaint turned pastoral: "Blind mouthes! that scarce themselves know how to hold / A Sheephook, or have learn'd ought else the least / That to the faithfull herdmans art belongs!" (119–21).

Thus Milton's piscatory procession of pagan gods concludes with St. Peter, the most famous Christian fisherman, delivering an invective against shepherds. Though admittedly awkward in this instance, the intermingling of the blue world with the green, the manner in which Fletcher concluded his *Eclogues* serves Milton's purpose well by reinforcing the poem's central grief—the singer's pastoral companion has been drowned. One cannot bury in green pastures a body lost at sea.

The final lines of "Lycidas" resound with the restrained optimism characteristic of the closing of pastoral songs, which are spent looking backward. The recollection of an idyllic past has occurred in an enchanted present—enchanted by the song itself (L. *in cantare*, "to sing upon"), the fellowship of companions, or, in this case, the vision of the poet. The procession of gods concluded and consolation provided, the singer hesitates to leave his present *locus*, which has transported him beyond both time and place. Neither shepherd nor fisher swain leaves such a place willingly. Inevitably, and ironically, it is time that bids them home. Thus comes the familiar descent of Phoebus and the consequent encroaching of shade, and an anonymous narrator tells us:

> And now the Sunne had stretch't out all the hills,
> And now was dropt into the western bay;
> At last he rose, and twitch't his Mantle blew,
> Tomorrow to fresh woods and pastures new.
>
> (190–93)

In his edition of Milton's works, Merritt Hughes suggests the closing of Virgil's first eclogue as a probable source of these lines.[16] While one can never doubt Milton's close eye to Virgil, a much more immediate source for these lines can be found in the closing lines of Fletcher's Eclogue VI, where, though the optimism is less restrained, we find his piscatory version of fresh woods and pastures new:

> Now let us home: for see, the creeping night
> Steals from those further waves upon the land.

To morrow shall we feast; then hand in hand
Free will we sing, and dance along the golden sand.

(26.7–10)

One other detail connects the closing lines of "Lycidas" with Fletcher's poem, and that is the curious garb of the uncouth swain. A "Mantle blew" may perhaps be appropriate dress in which to eulogize "the Genius of the shore," but it is clearly not typical pastoral clothing. Only one other reference to blue clothing appears, so far as I know, in pastoral poetry, English or otherwise, and that is in Fletcher's final eclogue, where "The fisher-boyes came driving up the stream; / Themselves in blue, and twenty sea-nymphs bright / In curious robes, that well the waves might seem" (VI.4.2–4). In Fletcher's eclogue these blue-robed swains meet with green-clad shepherds for a day of sport and rivalry. The two worlds intermingle in joyful rivalry. Here in "Lycidas," as I have noted already, the mixing of the two worlds serves a more profound and somber purpose. Clad in his blue mantle and watching the sun drop into the western bay, Milton's mournful swain, for all his singing to "th'Okes and rills," remains connected to his drowned friend whom he hopes, by song, to have kept from floating "upon his watry bear / Unwept . . ." (12–13).

It may be that tomorrow will indeed furnish new pastures and fresh woods, but the reader is doubtful. Having resided with the singer more in water than in fields, the reader has felt the green world vanishing, as it were, beneath his feet. Though masterful in its assimilation of pastoral and piscatory ingredients, Milton's "Lycidas" is clearly not the first of its kind. One wonders, though, watching the sun drop into the bay, if it is not the last, if what Spenser, Fletcher, and Milton understood and re-created as classical pastoral has never again been repeated.[17] The fields and academic cloisters along the River Cam were common to the youth of each of these pastoralists, and to each of their pastoral poems. Besides a common campus these three poets shared a common understanding that that campus could be the boundaried world they had inherited from Theocritus and Virgil—that the common losses of a literary classical past and a personal collegiate past could be recovered and held—green and undying—in the eclogue, the pastoralist's common and eternal field of play.

Notes

CHAPTER 1. THE PASTORALIST'S PAST

1. Even before Paul McLane's 1961 study of historical allegory in *Spenser's "Shepheardes Calender": A Study in Elizabethan Allegory* (University of Notre Dame Press, 1961), historical considerations of Renaissance pastoral poetry focused primarily on the Elizabethan court. More recently, New Historicists such as Louis Montrose have returned to the court-pastoral connection with renewed fervor. "The otiose love-talk of the shepherd," Montrose claims, "masks the busy negotiation of the courtier; the shepherd is a courtly poet prosecuting his courtship in pastoral forms" ("Eliza, Queen of Shepheardes, and the Pastoral of Power," *English Literary Renaissance* 10 [1980], 154). A similar notion is what kept McLane untangling anagrams in the first place. Less concerned with precisely who each of the shepherds represents, however, the New Historicist concerns himself instead with what those shepherds were up to, and what they were up to, of course, was not innocent bucolic conversation, but jockeying for power. Every shepherd is a would-be courtier and each shepherdess a must-be Elizabeth. Somewhat less insistent than Montrose, Stephen Greenblatt argues that Spenser's shepherds "are neither completely autonomous . . . nor entirely the creatures of the courtier's situation. There is a genuine doubleness about them, a mixture of outspokenness and diffidence" (*Representing the English Renaissance* [Berkeley: University of California Press, 1988], 166). Greenblatt's granting of at least some autonomy to the shepherd allows the pastoral poet something like a personal past, which, in the case of Spenser, among others, brings us most immediately to the gardens of Pembroke College at Cambridge University.

2. Peter Marinelli calls pastoral "the art of the backward glance" (*Pastoral* [London: Methuen and Co., Ltd, 1971], 9). Like Frank Kermode, he presents the case that pastoral poetry is essentially a nostalgic product, that the pastoralist lives and writes in one world (urban) and recollects another (rural). See Kermode's *English Pastoral Poetry, from the Beginnings to Marvell* (New York: Barnes and Noble, Inc., 1952), 14. This understanding of pastoral dates back at least as far as Quintilian, who, speaking of Theocritus, states: "*musa illa rustica et pastoralis non forum modo uerum ipsam etiam urbem reformidat*" (10.I.55) [that pastoral and rustic muse shuns not only the forum but even the very city itself].

3. Referring to Colin's departure from the pastoral in the December Eclogue of *The Shepheardes Calender*, E. K. writes: "Adiew delights is a conclusion of all. Where in sixe verses he comprehendeth briefly all that was touched in this booke. In the first verse his delights of youth generally" (211). All quotations from the *Calender* are taken from *The Yale Edition of the Shorter Poems of Edmund Spenser*, ed. William Orem et al. (New Haven: Yale University Press, 1989).

4. This oversimplification is not meant to exclude Spenser's other pastoral influences such as Marot, Ronsard, or Chaucer (or even possibly *Piers Plowman*), but merely to focus momentarily on the classical line in which Spenser placed himself, and by which pastoral, as a genre of English poetry, is traced.

5. Translation from Paul Alpers, *The Singer of the Eclogues* (Berkeley: University of California Press, 1979), 13.

6. Theocritus's depiction of Sicily as the famous one-eyed giant may have been a well-known allusion to its allegorical representation on coinage or a more deliberate extension of the poet's development of the pathetic fallacy. The allusion may also be a pointed political commentary or an internal poetic self reference. See commentary in A. S. F. Gow, ed., *Theocritus,* 2 vols. (Cambridge: Cambridge University Press, 1950, 2nd ed. 1952).

7. J. M. Edmonds, *The Greek Bucolic Poets* including the *Idylls* of Theocritus (Cambridge: Harvard University Press, 1977).

8. Steven Marx provides a succinct summary of Williams' escalator theory: "the good old days before the demise of country life elegaically recalled by the pastoralist usually turn out to be the days of his own youth—whether they transpired in the 20th, the 16th or the first century" ("The Pastoral Debate of Youth and Age: Genre and Life Cycle in Renaissance Poetry, with Special Reference to Edmund Spenser's *The Shepheardes Calendar*" [diss., Stanford University, 1981], 31).

9. Translation by Moses Hadas, *Three Greek Romances*, The Library of Liberal Arts (Bobbs-Merrill Co., Inc., 1953).

10. The broad-ranging interest in and exploration of pastoral ingredients by author and critic alike has continued to increase, seemingly without boundaries. This is exemplified, as well as anywhere, in twentieth-century American literature, where one finds Leslie Fiedler exploring Montana as a last unblemished pastoral, and articles such as Paul Rosenzweig's "[Henry] James's 'Special-Green Vision': *The Ambassadors* as Pastoral" Studies in the Novel 13:4 (winter 1981: 367–87).

11. The soundness of Schleiner's argument and its relevance to my own is addressed in chapter 2.

12. All quotations from *Piscatorie Eclogues* taken from Phineas Fletcher, *"The Purple Island; or, The Isle of Man": together with "Piscatorie Eclogs" and Other Poeticall Miscellanies* (Cambridge: University of Cambridge, 1633), 22 [Loyola University Special Collections].

13. David Masson, *The Life of John Milton Narrated in Connection with the Political, Ecclesiastical, and Literary History of His Time* (Cambridge: Macmillan and Co., 1859–94), 656.

14. Interestingly, pastoral poetry re-creates the good old days, but not nights. All of the evil connotations that belong to the dark arrive with the night and the discontented swains who mark time during the day dread even more the coming of the night.

15. The resemblance of this passage to the opening of the January Eclogue of *The Shepheardes Calender* was pointed out by Bain State Stewart in his article "A Borrowing from Spenser by Phineas Fletcher." *MLA* 56 (1941), 273–74.

16. Ironically, Piers's concerns do more to propel than prevent pastoral merriment. For as Poggioli correctly notes: "the pastoral operates at its best when there is some prudery left, when it still partakes of the inhibitions against which it raises

its protest or dissent" (*The Oaten Flute: Essays on Pastoral Poetry and the Pastoral Ideal* [Cambridge: Harvard University Press, 1975], 62).

17. Note here that time's arrival is in harmony with the poem's "action." In his familiar discussion of time's overt allegorical presence in the garden of Adonis (*The Poetry of "The Faerie Queene"* [Columbia: University of Missouri Press, 1982], 5–8), Paul Alpers points out Time's wicked dominion over Nature. Time's dominion in the examples we have looked at is far more subtle. Time is always present, even if unmeasured, and it is the measuring of time, rather than time itself, that threatens to destroy these pastoral worlds.

CHAPTER 2. THE CAMPUS

1. Easter Tuesday, this day was dedicated especially to a celebration of youth.

2. Recorded by one Fitzstephen and translated in F. M. Stenton's *Norman London* (London: Historical Association, 1934). Stenton tells of summer feast days that included "leaping, archery and wrestling, putting the stone and throwing the thonged javelin" (44).

3. William Soone writes in 1575 to a friend in Cologne: "none of them live out of the colleges in townsmen's houses" (Morgan, 187).

4. "Let them not attend the public shews of jugglers or actors, or presume to be present at Public exhibitions in churches, a theatre or stadia" (Gray, 155).

5. Just as the first Idyll of Theocritus laments the loss of Daphnis, so these English pastorals record the sorrowful loss of their most excellent singer. The world of the *Calender* suffers the departure of Colin Clout. The world of Fletcher's *Eclogues* is likewise disrupted by the departure of Thyrsil, and the loss of Lycidas (who "hath not left his peere") comprises Milton's pastoral elegy.

6. "A fellow offending in this article is to be fined a half-penny, a disciple may get off for a farthing" (Gray, 94).

7. In STATUTA REGINAE ELIZABETHAE. AN XII MO EDITA in *A Collection of Letters, Statutes, and Other Documents, from the Ms Library of Corpus Christi College*, ed. John Lamb (London: John W. Parker, 1838), scholars are instructed to continue their studies in the countryside in time of plague.

8. Alexander Judson, *The Life of Edmund Spenser*, in *The Works of Edmund Spenser: A Variorm Edition* (Baltimore: The Johns Hopkins University Press, 1945), 43. A. C. Hamilton suggests: "Since Spenser need not have remained in Cambridge during these years [between the time of his B.A. and M.A., 1573–1576], he may have visited the 'Northparts,' presumably the family home in Lancashire where he had a love affair with 'Rosalind' " (preface to *The Faerie Queene*, by Edmund Spenser, ed. A. C. Hamilton [Longman, 1977], viii).

9. In Longus's Greek pastoral romance, *Daphnis and Chloe*, the lovers return to the country to be married, so that their bucolic stepparents, their fellow herders, and even the goats themselves are able to take part in the wedding festivities. From thence forward the two lead a pastoral life. This rare allowance afforded to a pair who in the world of the city enjoy a status equivalent to prince and princess is clearly a happy exception to the normal pastoral course of things. More often than not, love consummation means a marriage without goats. In Book VI of *The Faerie Queene* Calidore brings Pastorella from the pastoral world to discover her old

courtly parents and her new courtly home. Likewise, in *As You Like It*, it is understood that after their marriage unions Rosalind and her companions will depart from Arden and return to the court.

10. The classic example of the shepherd-tutor is Meliboe, "that good old man," in Book VI of *The Faerie Queene*, who instructs Calidore in the essential ingredients of the pastoral world to which he (Meliboe) has returned after venturing into the corrupted world of the court (see canto ix.24.1–7).

11. In Poggioli's words: "the shepherd is neither a stoic nor a cynic, but . . . an epicurean and observes with natural spontaneity the ethics of that school" (8).

12. Students of all degrees were prohibited to "use any Daggers, Gunnes, Crossbowes or Stonebowes . . . either within their colledge or ye precincts of ye University, or abroad in the Country" (Cooper and Cooper, 2.539).

13. Judson, 26. The "principles" that kept Soone from Cambridge, Judson tells us, were his Roman Catholic leanings: "Soone knew whereof he wrote: a Cambridge man, he had served briefly as Regius Professor of the Civil Law, but had gone abroad in 1563 on account of his Catholic sympathies" (25).

14. Economics was not taught at Cambridge until the eighteenth century, and mathematics was introduced only in the mid-seventeenth century.

15. As if different colored gowns were not enough, Cambridge officials had to worry about priests, graduates, and younger students sporting such courtly fashions as "fair roses upon the shoe, long frizzled haire upon the head, broad spred Bands upon the shoulders and long large merchant Ruffs about the neck, with fayre feminine cuffs at the wrist" (Cooper and Cooper, 3.280).

16. In *An Abstract of the Composition between the University and Town of Cambridge* (London: Henricus Septimus, 1502), we learn that students' status as "privileged persons" included exemption from legal suits brought by citizens as well as a reprieve from detainment in jail after an arrest: "he shall have vii days to bring a certificate under any seal of the chancellor, vice-chancellor or his lieutenant, that he is a scholar and upon such certificate shall be immediately discharged" (Lamb, 2).

17. This title is given to Fletcher by Francis Quarles in his prefatory verse in the 1633 edition of Fletcher's works: "To the ingenious composer of This Pastorall, The Spencer of this age."

CHAPTER 3. COLIN CLOUT'S "STAYED STEPS"

1. Quotations from *The Shepheardes Calender* are taken from *The Yale Edition of the Shorter Poems of Edmund Spenser*, ed. William A. Oram et al. (New Haven: Yale University Press, 1989). Quotations from *The Faerie Queene* are from the edition of J. C. Smith (1909), reprinted as *The Faerie Queene*, ed. A. C. Hamilton (London: Longman, 1977).

2. This particular description is David L. Miller's, in his insightful article "Authorship, Anonymity, and *The Shepheardes Calender*," *MLQ* 40 (1979), but it could have come from any number of recent and not-so-recent readings of the *Calender* which, while offering excellent insight into how Spenser fashioned his poetic career, depend upon a rather literal understanding of Colin Clout's aging, which is then undone in Book VI of *The Faerie Queene*. In making my present

argument I have given consideration not just to Miller's piece, but also Richard Helgerson, "The New Poet Presents Himself: Spenser and the Idea of a Literary Career," *PMLA* 93 (1978), David R. Shore, *Spenser and the Poetics of Pastoral* (Kingston: McGill-Queen's University Press, 1985), and most recently Louise Schleiner's "Spenser's 'E. K.' as Edmund Kent (Kenned / of Kent): Kyth (Couth), Kissed, and Kunning-Conning," *ELR* 20 (1990).

3. Creighton Gilbert, "When Did A Man in the Renaissance Grow Old?" in *Studies In The Renaissance*, vol. 14 (New York: Publishers of the Renaissance Society of America, 1967). In addressing the tropological significance of aging, Gilbert does not negate the actual fact of aging, nor deny that a forty-year-old man in the sixteenth century was physiologically "older" than a forty-year-old in the late twentieth century. Recognition of historical changes in actual aging through the centuries helps us account, in large part, for a Renaissance man's "early" preoccupation with aging. In turn, however, the physiological reality of aging in any century neither prevents nor accounts for its use as an artistic convention. Gilbert's examination of old age as a trope does not supplant old age as a fact. A man in the Renaissance—like a man now—had a variety of reasons for describing himself as old. Neither Gilbert in his argument, nor I in my present one, deny that one of those reasons may have been because he was, in fact, old.

4. The word *mot* describes the particular kind of emblem used by Spenser in the *Calender*. A type of *impressa*, the mot is a short sentence of poesy, usually grave or amorous in tone, which may be used without figures. See Paolo Giovio, *The Worthy Tract of Paulus Joyius*, trans. Samuel Daniel (1585; reprint, Delmar, NY: Scholar's Facsimiles & Reprints, 1976).

5. John Bender, *Spenser and Literary Pictorialism* (Princeton: Princeton University Press, 1972), 156.

6. Miller calls the poem "a completely self-conscious poetic debut" (219). Helgerson notes that "Spenser's poetic self-image could in fact be described with some accuracy as a compound of Petrarch, Mantuan, Ariosto, Tasso, and Virgil" (895).

7. Compare the *OED*. definition of stay, sb2–1: "Something that supports or steadies something else" (as early as 1515), with sb3–1: "The action of stopping or bringing to a stand or pause; the fact of being brought to a stand or delayed; a stoppage, arrest, or suspension of action; a check, set-back" (examples from as early as 1537); sb3–2: "control; restraint; self-control" (1556), and sb3–3: "A coming to a stand; a cessation of progress or action" (1530).

8. *OED*. definitions sb3–4 and 10.

9. Howard Hibbard, *Michelangelo*, 2nd ed. (New York: Harper & Row, 1974), 56.

10. Hibbard's remarks are, I think, more aptly applied to the Bacchus whose feet and posture are more clearly contrapposta.

11. *Devices Heroiques*, ed. John Horden Menston (1557; reprint, Scolar Press, 1971). This book, compiled by Claude Paradin, was an expansion of the first edition printed in 1551. Many subsequent editions followed the 1557 printing.

12. Hadrianus Junius, *Emblemata* (1565; Menston reprint, Scolar Press, 1972).

13. Interestingly, Wind traces the interlace, contra-distinction, and general choreography of the Graces' dance to passages from Horace and Seneca. Spenser's familiarity with such ekphrastic possibilities would likely derive as much from reading as from viewing.

14. Piers's familiar advice to the discouraged Cuddye in October of the *Calender*:

> Abandon then the base and viler clowne,
> Lyft up thy selfe out of the lowly dust:
> And sing of bloody Mars, of wars, of giusts.
> Turne thee to those, that weld the awful crowne,
> To doubted Knights, whose woundlesse armour rusts,
> And helmes unbruzed wexen dayly browne.

(1.37–42)

15. From *The European Emblem: Towards an Index*, ed. Peter M. Daly (Waterloo, Ont.: Wilfred Laurier University Press, 1980). Printed by Peacham in London in 1612, this figure of Capriccio has numerous precedents in the sixteenth century, and Spenser was undoubtedly familiar with some version of this figure.

16. *OED.*: 1. "A sudden sportive or fantastic motion."

17. In Book Three of *Amores*, the poet sees Elegy appear "limping, one foot short" (1.7). Then Tragedy appears, "And on her feet high Lydian buskins bound" (13). Tragedy scolds the poet, telling him "your youth's been spent on young men's poetry. / I'm Roman Tragedy, now make me famous, / You know my rules and you will rise to me" (28–30). *Ovid: The Love Poems*, trans. A. D. Melville (Oxford: Oxford University Press, 1990).

18. This notion is by no means an original one. One fairly recent and insightful version of this idea is Richard Mallette's "Spenser's Portrait of the Artist in *The Shepheardes Calender* and *Colin Clouts Come Home Againe*," *SEL, 1500–1900* 19 (1979): 19–41. As his title suggests, Mallette finds that in these two works by Spenser "Colin Clout's progress rehearses the classic ascent of the Neoplatonic soul" (22). Curiously, however, Mallette leaves out of his investigation Colin's most "classic ascent" as well as his most extravagant Neoplatonic vision, namely the shepherd's piping upon Mount Acidale in Book VI of *The Faerie Queene*.

19. His chase of the Blatant Beast takes him from the court to cities, from cities to towns, from towns to country, from country to private farms, from private farms to fields, and from fields to Mount Acidale.

20. Readers who assume that Colin Clout's beloved is Rosalind would seem to negate any real connection between *The Shepheardes Calender* and the present book even while they seek to make one. Such readers would reverse Rosalind's resolute scorn in the same way in which readers reverse Colin's aging. Why should Rosalind have come around to be Colin's true love since *The Shepheardes Calender*? This "jolly Shepheards lasse" makes Colin "pipe so merrily or never none." Rosalind, on the other hand, had scorned shepherds' songs and put a violent stop to Colin's singing.

21. "All thinges perish and come to theyr last end, but workes of learned wits and monuments of Poetry abide for ever."

CHAPTER 4. "SHEPHEARDES DELIGHTS"

1. Published in 1498, the Latin eclogues of Battista Spagnuolo were familiarly called "Mantuan" after the poet's birthplace. Written from an "austerely clerical"

point of view (Battista joined a Carmelite monastery before the eclogues were completed), the eclogues possess a "pervasive moral tone, religious in flavor" (Kennedy, 150), and thus serve as a suitable contrast to Arcadian pastoral.

2. I recognize here the slippery nature of such a term as this. I might instead include the qualification "pastoral worldviews." The Arcadian shepherd conceives of his world as a pastoral world, as I have defined it in the first three chapters (outside of time and place, containing the joys of youth). The Mantuan shepherd's world does not differ much from yours or mine. He accepts man's fallen state and envisions the "pastoral" world as the hapless circumstance of his ill-spent youth.

3. My bringing together of Cullen's terms with those used by Berger demonstrates not only the similarity of their two readings, but an essential fact about the poem's narrative structure: its basic dichotomy of pleasure and loss of pleasure. This dichotomy is further borne out as I trace the term "delight" through the poem.

4. Ironically, David Miller, who also regards Colin as "a worldes child" because of his "surrender to nature," sees Colin emerging, not as England's heroic poet, as Hamilton does, but "as Spenser's definitive 'worldes child,' his fate an ironic completion of partial instances of the type" (234).

5. "Hobbinol is a fained country name, whereby, it being so commune and vsuall seemeth to be hidden the person of some his very speciall and most familiar freend, whom he entirely and extraordinarily beloued, as peraduenture shall be more largely declared hereafter."

6. Harvey's own account of his misfortunes in his letters of appeal to Master Young provides us the most revealing versions of both his circumstance and his character.

7. Harvey's ill opinion of his own "Verlayes" is illustrated in his letter of 1579. Harvey, troubled that Spenser has published without permission Harvey's first attempts at English verse, writes to Spenser that the only way he can make amends is to send to him by the next carrier to Stourbridge Fair "the clippings of your thris honorable mustachyoes and subboscoes to overshadow and to cover my blushinge" (*Letter-Book*, x).

8. Indications are that this may be a younger Thenot, rather than the Thenot of the February Eclogue. In regards to the role he plays in the eclogue, his age is of little consequence one way or the other.

9. A term that "E. K." tells us means stranger. It may even mean enemy.

10. This is essentially the same message Cuddie delivers to Thenot, albeit with less grace.

11. Not only the idea of depicting the joys through loss but this very departure speech will be imitated by Phineas Fletcher at the end of his second eclogue in his *Piscatorie Eclogues*.

CHAPTER 5. "UNGRATEFUL CHAME!"

1. Osgood gathers this information from Holinshed, who goes on to say that the River Cam receives "by and by the Stoure, or Sture (at whose bridge the most famous mart in England is yearlie holden and kept)" (I.174). Holinshed is referring to the Stourbridge Fair, which occurred on the lower side of Cambridge. The Stoure has since been lost in the ditches.

2. Fletcher openly acknowledges his pastoral debt to Virgil and Spenser in canto vi, stanza 5 of *The Purple Island*:

> Two shepherds most I love with just adoring.
> That Mantuan swain, who chang'd his slender reed
> To trumpet's martial voice, and war's loud roaring,
> From Corydon to Turnus' daring deed;
>   And next our homebred Colin's sweetest firing;
>   Their steps not following close, but far admiring;
> To lacquey one of these is all my pride's aspiring.

3. *The Purple Island* was published, along with *Piscatorie Eclogues*, in 1633. Both works appeared in volume I of the two-volume edition of *Giles and Phineas Fletcher: Poetical Works*. Examination of the three epics *The Faerie Queene*, *The Purple Island*, and *Paradise Lost* occupies the bulk of Herbert Cory's study of Phineas Fletcher in "Spenser, the School of the Fletchers, and Milton," *University of California Publications in Modern Philology* 2, no. 5 (1912), 311 ff, and is the subject of comparisons made between the three poets since Cory's time.

4. The clique included Fletcher's brother Giles, John Tompkins, William Cappell, Edmond Cook, and William Woodford (Kastor, 80), all of whom show up in Fletcher's poetry bearing pastoral pseudonyms.

5. Note that the only other depiction of a fisher in *The Faerie Queene* is Malengrin, the false fisher of men in Book V who "used to fish for fools on the dry shore" (V.ix.ii).

6. "Pastoral life," Renato Poggioli points out, "may reserve . . . a small place for the fisherman, if he does not risk his life on the high seas, but throws his net not too far from shore or sinks his line into a nearby pond or brook. Such a fisherman is twin brother to the shepherd" (*The Oaten Flute: Essays on Pastoral Poetry and the Pastoral Ideal* [Cambridge: Harvard University Press, 1975], 7).

7. All quotations from Fletcher are taken from *"The Purple Island; or, The Isle of Man": Together with "Piscatorie Eclogs" and Other Poeticall Miscellanies* (Cambridge: the Printers to the University of Cambridge, 1633) [Loyola University Special Collections].

8. Simone Dorangeon notes that Fletcher "réussit comme son maître italien à 'pastoraliser', c'est-à-dire à utiliser les thèmes canevas et motifs Virgiliens, tout en substituant au système bucolique traditionnel un système cohérent de 'signes' empruntés au monde de la pêche" [succeeded, just as his Italian master, to 'pastoralize,' that is, use the themes, images and virgilian motifs, all of which were incorporated into the traditional bucolic system, à system full of 'signs' imprinted in the world of fish] ("De Phineas Fletcher à Izaak Walton: Quelques notes sur la transmission du symbolisme piscatorial," *Bulletin de la société d'études Anglo-Americaines des XVIIe et XVIIIe siècles* 7 [November 1978]: 63–64).

9.   Dumque alii notosque sinus piscosaque circum
> Aequora collustrant flammis aut linea longe
> Retia captivosque trahunt ad litora pisces,
> Ipse per obscuram meditatur carmina noctem.

(II.4–7)

10. *Celadon.*   Dic mihi (nam Baulis, verum si rettulit Aegon,
Bis senos vos, Mopse, dies tenuere procellae)
Quid tu, quid Chromis interea, quid vester Iolas,
Dum Notus insultat pelago, dum murmurat unda . . .
Mopsus.   Quid nostrae facerent ingrata per otia Musae,
O Celadon? Neque tum conchas impune licebat
Per scopulos, non octipedes tentare paguros;
Jam fragilem in sicco munibant saxa phaselum
Raraque per longos pendebant retia remos;
Ante pedes cistaeque leves hamique jacebant
Et calami nassaeque et viminei labyrinthi.

(III.1–4; 6–12)

11. The departure of one swain from another is a pastoral convention that can be traced at least as far back as Eclogue I of Virgil.

12. As Simone Dorangeon explains: "De même que, depuis le moine Radbert au Moyen Age, depuis Pétrarque et depuis Spenser, les auteurs de pastorales allégoriques justifiaient l'équation berger = homme d' église, chef spirituel et religieux préoccupé du bien-être de ceux qui l'entourent en invoquant l'autorité de la Bible et en citant le Chapitre X de l'Evangile selon St Jean et la parabole du Bon Pasteur, telle que St Luc nous la rapporte, de même Phineas Fletcher prêta le travesti de pêcheur aux hommes chargés d'une mission salvatrice en remontant à l'épisode du Christ qui choisit quatre de ses apôtres parmi les pêcheurs, prit leurs âmes à son divin 'hamecon' et leur demanda de poursuivre à travers l'humanité une pêche génératrice d'espérance" (64–65) [Ever since the Monk Radbert during the Middle Ages, and Petrarch and Spenser, authors of pastoral allegories have justified the equation of shepherd = clergyman, a spiritual and religious leader preoccupied with the well-being of those around him by invoking the authority of the Bible and by citing Chapter X of the Gospel according to St. John and the parable of the Good Shepherd, such as St. Luke recounts it to us. Just so Phineas Fletcher lends the role of fisher to men charged with a saving mission by going back to the episode of Christ who chose four of his apostles from amont fishermen, caught their souls on his divine 'hook' and asked them to pursue among men a fishing expedition generating hope].

13. The general curriculum at Cambridge remained largely unchanged from 1550 to 1850. First-year disciples read dialectic and the best elements of Euclid. In the second year they engaged in logic. In the third year, they studied ethics, politics, and rhetoric (including classical poetry), and in the fourth year the physical sciences. A first-year student had to translate Demosthenes into Latin and Cicero into Greek.

14. That the "Prince of fishers" represents Peter, not Christ, is made clear later when Christ is referred to as "the King of Seas."

CHAPTER 6. "THE UNCOUTH SWAIN"

1. As Cory puts it: "Apart from the Greek and Latin poets and from the great books of philosophy and religion, Milton's literary lineage is to be traced from his master Spenser and from the strange perverted works of a group of poets who had

much greater academic vogue than is now generally understood, the School of the Fletchers ("The School," 344). In his characterization of Fletcher's works as strange and perverse, Cory echoes a common opinion of Fletcher's *The Purple Island* in particular.

2. The words belong to Paul Alpers, who offers a good summation of the difficulties that modern critics have with the poem, difficulties that "were first raised by Samuel Johnson," whom he says "was disturbed by the gap between the machinery of the poem and the feeling it purports to express. Where he demanded sincerity, the modern critic seeks authenticity." Alpers notes that Johnson "may be thought to have established the tradition that excellent critics write weakly or perversely on this poem" (" 'Lycidas' and Modern Criticism," *ELH* 49, no. 2 [1982], 469).

3. As quoted by Joseph Wittreich, "From Pastoral to Prophesy: The Genres of 'Lycidas,' " *Milton Studies* 13 (1979), 59.

4. Spenser "would have been only 27 in 1579. That is if he were born in 1552: for all we know, he may have been born two years earlier" ("Grene Path," 4).

5. A kind interpretation of Milton's collegiate nickname attributes it to his extremely youthful appearance. As Gray points out, however, its origins likely stem from his classmates' more cruel opinion of the young poet's femininity (Arthur Gray, *Cambridge University: An Episodical History* [Cambridge: Cambridge University Press, 1926]).

6. Prose translation by Hughes in John Milton, *Complete Poems and Major Prose*, ed. Merritt Y. Hughes (New York: Macmillan, 1985), 8.

7. In quoting from the poem in this chapter, I use the 1638 edition of "Lycidas" as it appeared in the memorial volume *Justa Edovardo King*. I do this not for any textual superiority this earlier version possesses (the revisions made for the 1645 edition are generally slight but sure), but because it is nearest to the occasion of Milton's idyllic remembrance of Edward King and Cambridge.

8. *Apology for Smectymnuus*, as quoted in Masson, 271.

9. Ibid., 269.

10. *Defensio Secunda*, as quoted in Masson, 269.

11. See Masson, 562–63 for an explicit, if somewhat fanciful, description of life at Horton in all four seasons.

12. "The range of pastoral is indeed narrow," Johnson writes in *Rambler* 36, "for though nature itself, philosophically considered, be exhaustible, yet its general effects on the eye and on the ear are uniform, and incapable of much variety of description" ("Pastoral Poetry I and II" [*Rambler* #36 and #37], in Yale edition of *The Work of Samuel Johnson*, ed. W. J. Bate and Albrecht R. Strauss [New Haven: Yale Univ. Press, 1969] 197). Johnson concedes that as each age makes discoveries of new plants or new modes of culture, pastoral may be revived and "receive . . . once in a century a scene somewhat varied" (197). As Johnson describes it, the finest pastoral poet would be a well-traveled and metrically inclined horticulturalist.

13. Varney cites the *OED* definition, 5c: "strange, uneasy, at a loss" and notes that "Milton uses the word 'uncouth' nine times in his verse, and on six of these occasions it is appropriate to see the use as enhanced by implications of solitude, loneliness and being disconsolate" ("Milton's 'Uncouth Swain,' " *Notes and Queries* 29 [1982], 75).

14. The other group of deliberate "Spenserians" was headed by William Browne, former Oxford don, well known as early as 1614. The Fletchers obviously were the more immediate influence on Milton, being, like Spenser himself, Cambridge poets.

15. Cory writes: "In *Lycidas* this bitterness [against the clergy] is more unruly and is, in this case, plausibly traceable, in part, to the influence of Spenser. At least as early as Thomas Warton, critics have pointed out the similarity between the abusive digression of religious polemics in "Lycidas" and janglings of Piers and Palinode in the May eclogue of *The Shepheardes Calender*. Mantuan and Petrarch had attacked bad clergy in their eclogues. But their influence is more remote than that of Milton's chosen master. Moreover, Spenser's eclogue was the specific attack of Protestant upon Catholic. In this he was followed by some of his imitators, notably Phineas Fletcher, in his *Appolyonists* and in his *Piscatorie Eclogues* (1633). We have specific evidence that Spenser's abusive eclogues appealed particularly to Milton" (358).

16. The lines to which Hughes refers are these:

> *Melibee.* Go now, my goats; once happy flock, move on.
> No more shall I, stretched out in a cavern green,
> Watch you, far off, on brambly hillsides hang.
> I'll sing no songs, nor shepherd you when you
> Browse on the flowering shrubs and bitter willows.
> *Tityrus.* Still, you could take your rest with me tonight,
> Couched on green leaves: there will be apples ripe,
> Soft roasted chestnuts, plenty of pressed cheese.
> Already rooftops in the distance smoke,
> And lofty hills let fall their lengthening shade.

(I.74–83)

I have used Paul Alpers's translation.

17. In the eighteenth century Alexander Pope accomplishes four "pastorals," seemingly for pastoral's sake. By the nineteenth century romantic poets have become interested in landscapes as landscapes and shepherds as shepherds. By the time one arrives at, say, Thoreau's bean field on Walden Pond, a deliberately artificial and ekphrastic re-creation of nature seems forever improbable, Frost and Yeats being two possible modern exceptions to the otherwise "realistic" explorations of nature.

Bibliography

Alpers, Paul. "Convening and Convention in Pastoral Poetry." *NLH* 14(1981): 277 ff.

———. "The Eclogue Tradition and the Nature of Pastoral." *College English* 34 no. 3 (1972): 352–71.

———. " 'Lycidas' and Modern Criticism." *ELH* 49, no. 2 (1982): 468–96.

———. *The Poetry of "The Faerie Queene."* Columbia: University of Missouri Press, 1982.

———. "What is Pastoral?" *CI* 8 (1982): 437–60.

———. *What is Pastoral?* Chicago: Chicago University Press, 1997.

Attwater, Aubrey. *Pembroke College, Cambridge: A Short History.* Cambridge, Cambridge University Press, 1936.

Baldwin, E. C. "Milton and Phineas Fletcher." *Journal of English and Germanic Philology* 33 (1934): 544–46.

Baldwin, Robert G. "Controlling Ideas in the Poetry of Phineas Fletcher, 1582–1650." Ph.D. diss., University of Toronto, 1957.

———. "Phineas Fletcher: His Modern Readers and His Renaissance Ideas." *Philological Quarterly* 40 (1961): 470.

Berger, Harry. "The Aging Boy: Paradise and Parricide in Spenser's *Shepheardes Calender.*" In *Poetic Traditions of the English Renaissance*, edited by Mack Maynard and Lord George deForest, 25–46. New Haven: Yale University Press, 1982.

———. "Orpheus, Pan, and the Poetics of Misogyny: Spenser's Critique of Pastoral, Love and Art." *ELH* 50 (1983): 27–61.

Bouchard, Gary M. "From Campus to Campus: English University Life and the Renaissance Pastoral." *Journal of the Rocky Mountain Medieval and Renaissance Association* 12 (1991): 105–28.

———. "Phineas Fletcher: The Piscatory Link between Spenserian and Miltonic Pastoral." *Studies in Philology* 89, no. 2 (spring 1992): 232–43.

———. "Stayed Steps: Colin Clout's Slow Hastening into Riper Years." *Studies in Iconography* 15 (1993): 197–214.

Bourdette, Robert E. "Mourning Lycidas: The Poem of the Mind in the Act of Finding What Will Suffice." *Essays in Literature* 2 (1984): 11–20.

Brown, James Neil. "Elizabethan Pastoralism and Renaissance Platonism." *AUMLA* 44 (1975): 246–67.

Bush, Douglas. *English Literature in the Earlier Seventeenth Century, 1600–1660.* Oxford: Oxford University Press, 1945.

Camden, William Britian. *The History of the Most Renowned and Victorius Princess Elizabeth, Late Queen of England*, reprint Chicago: University of Chicago Press, 1970.

Camden, William Britian. *Tr. Philemon Holland*. London: n.p., 1610.

A Catalogue of the Manuscripts Preserved in the Library of the University of Cambridge. Cambridge: Cambridge University Press, 1867.

Chambers, Edmund K. *English Pastorals*. Freeport, N.Y.: Books for Libraries Press, 1969.

Cioranescu, Alexandre. *Vie de Jacques Amyot*. Paris: Librarie E. Droz, 1941.

Cody, Richard. *The Landscape of the Mind*. Oxford: Clarendon Press, 1969.

Cooper, Charles Henry, and John William Cooper. *Annals of Cambridge*. Vols. 2 and 3. Cambridge: Warick & Co., 1842–1908.

Cooper, Helen. *Pastoral: Medieval into Renaissance*. Ipswich: Brewer, Rowman, and Littlefield, 1977.

Cory, Herbert E. "The Golden Age of the Spenserian Pastoral." *PMLA* 25 (1910): 241–67.

———. "Spenser, the School of the Fletchers, and Milton." *University of California Publications in Modern Philology* 2, no. 5 (1912): 311 ff.

Courthope, W. J. A. *History of English Poetry*. London: Fuller Worthies Library, 1869.

Cullen, Patrick. *Spenser, Marvell, and Renaissance Pastoral*. Cambridge: Harvard University Press, 1970.

Curtius, Ernst Robert. *European Literature of the Latin Middle Ages*. Translated by Willard R. Trask. New York: Harper and Row, 1953.

Davis, Robert L. "That Two-Handed Engine and the Consolation of 'Lycidas.' " *Milton Quarterly* 20 (1986): 44–48.

Davis, Walter R. *A Map of Arcadia: Sidney's Romance in Its Tradition*. London: Yale University Press, 1965.

Dorangeon, Simone. "De Phineas Fletcher à Izaak Walton: Quelques notes sur la la transmission du symbolisme piscatorial." *Bulletin de la société d'études Anglo-Americaines des XVIIe et XVIIIe siècles* 7 (November 1978): 63–74.

Durr, Allen. "Spenser's Calender of Christian Time." *ELH* 24 (1957): 294–95.

Edmonds, J. M. *The Greek Bucolic Poets*, (including the "*Idylls*" of Theocritus.) Cambridge: Harvard University Press, 1977.

Empson, William. *Some Versions of Pastoral*. New York: New Directions Press, 1974.

Ettin, Andrew V. *Literature and the Pastoral*. New Haven: Yale University Press, 1984.

Evans, J. Martin. *The Road from Horton: Looking Backwards in "Lycidas"*. English Literary Series. Victoria, BC: University of Victoria, 1983.

Fletcher, Giles, and Phineas Fletcher. *Giles and Phineas Fletcher: Poetical Works*. Edited by Frederick S. Boas. Cambridge: Cambridge University Press, 1909.

Fletcher, Phineas. *A Father's Testament*. London: H. Mortlock, 1670.

————. *Joy in Tribulation; or, Consolations of Afflicted Spirits*. London: I. Boler, 1632.

————. *"Piscatorie Eclogues," with Other Poetic Miscellanies*. Edinburgh: A. Kincaid and W. Creech; London: T. Cadell, 1771.

————. *The Poems of Phineas Fletcher*. Edited by Alexander B. Grosart. London: Fuller Worthies Library, 1869.

————. *The Purple Island: A Poem*. Edited by Henry Headley. London: Burton and Briggs, 1816.

————. *"The Purple Island; or, The Isle of Man": Together with "Piscatorie Eclogs" and Other Poeticall Miscellanies*. Cambridge: the Printers to the University of Cambridge, 1633 [Loyola University Special Collections].

————. *Sicelides: A Piscatory, As It Hath Been Acted in King's Colledge, in Cambridge*. London: Printed by IN to William Steares, 1631.

Freeman, Rosemary. *English Emblem Books*. New York: Octagon Books, 1966.

Gilbert, Creighton. "When Did A Man in the Renaissance Grow Old?" In *Studies in the Renaissance*. Vol. 14. New York: Publishers of the Renaissance Society of America, 1967.

Gow, A. S. F., ed., *Theocritus*, 2 vols. Cambridge: Cambridge University Press, 1950; 2nd ed. 1952.

Gransden, K. W. "The Pastoral Alternative." *Arethusa* 3 (1970): I:103–21; 2:177–96.

Gray, Arthur. *Cambridge University: An Episodical History* [new Edition of *Cambridge and Its Story*, 1912]. Cambridge: Cambridge University Press, 1926.

Greenblatt, Stephen. "Invisible Bullets: Renaissance Authority and Its Subversion." In *Glyph: Johns Hopkins Textual Studies*. Baltimore: The Johns Hopkins University Press, 1981.

————. *Renaissance Self-Fashioning*. Chicago: University of Chicago Press, 1980.

————. *Representing the English Renaissance*. Berkeley: University of California Press, 1988.

Greg, W. W. *Pastoral Poetry and Pastoral Drama*. London: A. H. Bollen, 1906.

Grundy, Joan. *The Spenserian Poets*. New York: St. Martin's Press, 1969.

Haber, Judith. *Pastoral and the Poetics of Self-Contradiction: Theocritus to Marvell*. Cambridge: Cambridge University Press, 1994.

Hager, Alan. *Shakespeare's Political Animal: Schema and Schemata in the Canon*. Newark: University of Delaware Press, 1990.

Hamilton, A. C. "The Argument of *The Shepheardes Calender*." *ELH* 36 (1969): 105 ff.

————. "The Grene Path Way to Lyfe": Spenser's *Shepheardes Calender* as Pastoral." In *The Elizabethan Theatre VIII*, edited by George Hibbard, 1–21. Port Credit, Ontario: Meany, 1982.

Hanford, J. H. *A Milton Handbook*. New York: Crofts, 1946.

Harvey, Gabriel. *Letter-Book of Gabriel Harvey, 1573–1580*. Edited by Edward John Long Scott. Printed by John Wolfe Westminister: n.p.: The Camden Society, 1884.

————. *Marginalia*. Collected and edited by G. C. Moore Smith Stratford-upon-Avon: Shakespeare Head Press, 1913.

————. *A New Letter of Notable Contents*. London: n.p., 1593.

Helgerson, Richard. "The New Poet Presents Himself: Spenser and the Idea of a Literary Career." *PMLA* 93 (1978) 893–911.

Heninger, S. K., Jr. "The Renaissance Perversion of Pastoral." *JHI* 22 (1961): 354–61.

Heywood, James. *Early Cambridge University and College Statutes*. London: Henry G. Bohn, 1855.

Heywood, James, and Thomas Wright, eds. *Cambridge University Transactions during the Puritan Controversies of the 16th and 17th Centuries*. 2 vols. London: Henry G. Bohn, 1854.

Hibbard, Howard (p. 142).

Hieatt, Charles W. "The Integrity of Pastoral: A Basis for Definition." *Genre* 5 (1972): 1–30.

Hunter, William B. *The English Spenserians: The Poetry of Giles Fletcher, George Wither, Michael Drayton, Phineas Fletcher, and Henry More*. Salt Lake City: University of Utah Press, 1977.

————. *A Milton Encyclopedia*. Vol. 3. Lewisburg, PA: Bucknell University Press, 1978.

Johnson, Barbara. "Fiction and Grief: The Pastoral Idiom of Milton's 'Lycidas.' " *Milton Quarterly* 18, no. 3 (1984): 69–76.

Johnson, Samuel. *Lives of the English Poets*. Edited by George Birkbeck Hill. Oxford: Clarendon Press, 1968.

————. "Pastoral Poetry I and II" (*Rambler* #36 and #37). In Yale ed. of *The Works of Samuel Johnson*, edited by W. J. Bate and Albrecht B. Strauss. New Haven: Yale University Press, 1969.

Judson, Alexander C. "The Life of Edmund Spenser." In *The Works of Edmond Spenser: A Variorum Edition*. Baltimore: The Johns Hopkins University Press, 1945.

The Kalender of Shepherds. The edition of Paris 1503 in photographic facsimile. A faithful reprint of R. Pyson's edition of London 1506. Edited with a critical introduction and glossary by H. Oskar Sommer, Ph.D. London: Kegan Paul, Trench, Trubner & Co. Ltd., 1892.

Kastor, Frank S. *Giles and Phineas Fletcher*. Boston: Twayne, 1978.

Kearney, Hugh. *Scholars and Gentlemen, Universities and Society in Pre-Industrial Britain, 1500–1700*. London: Faber and Faber, 1970.

Kegel-Brinkgreve, E. *The Echoing Woods: Bucolic and Pastoral from Theocritus to Wordsworth*. Philadelphia: John Benjamins Publishing Company, 1990.

Kennedy, William. *Jacopo Sannazaro and the Uses of Pastoral*. London: University Press of New England, 1983.

Kermode, Frank. *English Pastoral Poetry, from the Beginnings to Marvell*. New York: Barnes and Noble, 1952.

King, John N. "Spenser's *Shepheardes Calender* and Protestant Pastoral Satire." In *Renaissance Genres: Essays on Theory, History, and Interpretation,* edited by Barbara Kiefer Lewalski, 369–98. Cambridge: Harvard University Press.

Lamb, J., ed. *A Collection of Letters, Statutes, and Other Documents from the Ms Library of Corpus Christi College*. (London: John W. Parker), 1838.

Lambert, Ellen Zetzel. *Placing Sorrow: A Study of the Pastoral Elegy Convention from Theocritus to Milton*. Chapel Hill: University of North Carolina Press, 1976.

Lane, Robert. *Shepheards Devises*. Athens: University of Georgia Press, 1993.

Langdale, Adam Barnett. *Phineas Fletcher, Man of Letters, Science, and Divinity*. New York: Columbia University Press, 1937.

Lerner, Laurence. *The Uses of Nostalgia: Studies in Pastoral Poetry*. New York: Schocken Books, 1972.

Longus. *Daphnis and Chloe*. In *Three Greek Romances*, edited by Moses Hadas. Indianapolis: Bobbs-Merrill Educational Publishing, 1981.

MacCaffrey, Isabel. "Allegory and Pastoral in *The Sheapherdes Calender*." *ELH* 36 (1969): 88 ff.

———. " 'Lycidas': The Poet in a Landscape." In *The Lyric and Dramatic Milton*, edited by Joseph H. Summers, 84–91. New York: Columbia University Press 1965.

McConica, James. "Scholars and Commoners in Renaissance Oxford." In *The University and Society*. Vol. 1. Edited by Lawrence Stone. London: Oxford University Press, 1975.

McLane, Paul E. *Spenser's "Shepheardes Calender": A Study in Elizabethan Allegory*. Notre Dame, Ind.: University of Notre Dame Press, 1961.

Mallette, Richard. *Spenser, Milton and Renaissance Pastoral*. Lewisburg, PA: Bucknell University Press, 1981.

———. "Spenser's Portrait of the Artist in *The Shepheardes Calender* and *Colin Clouts Come Home Againe*." *Studies in English Literature, 1500–1900* 19 (1979): 19–41.

Marinelli, Peter V. *Pastoral*. London: Methuen and Co., 1971.

Marx, Steven Rudolph. " 'Fortunate Senex': The Pastoral of Old Age." *SEL* 25 (1985): 21–44.

———. "The Pastoral Debate of Youth and Age: Genre and Life Cycle in Renaissance Poetry, with Special Reference to Edmund Spenser's *The Shepheardes Calender*." Diss., Stanford University, 1981.

———. *Youth against Age: Generational Strife in Renaissance Poetry*. American University Studies IV: English Language and Literature, vol. 21. New York: Peter Lang Publishing, 1986.

Masson, David. *The Life of John Milton Narrated in Connection with the Political, Ecclesiastical, and Literary History of His Time*. Cambridge: Macmillan and Co., 1859–94.

Mayor, J. E. B. *Cambridge in the Seventeenth Century*. Cambridge: Cambridge University Press, 1856.

Miller, David L. "Authorship, Anonymity, and *The Shepheardes Calender*." *Modern Language Quarterly* 40 (1979): 219–36.

Milton, John. *Complete Poems and Major Prose*. Edited by Merritt Y. Hughes. New York: Macmillan, 1985.

————. "Lycidas." In *JUSTA Edovardo King Naufrago, ab Amicis Moerentibus, Amoris &. Si Recte Calculum Ponas, Ubique Naufragium Est. Pet. Arb. Cantabrigiae.* Cambridge: Apud T. Buck and R. Daniel, 1638.

Montrose, Louis Adrian. "Eliza, Queene of Shepheardes, and the Pastoral of Power." *English Literary Renaissance* 10 (1980): 153–82.

————. "Of Gentlemen and Shepherds: The Politics of Elizabethan Pastoral Form." *ELH* 50 (1983): 415–59.

Morgan, Victor. "Cambridge University and 'The Country,' 1560–1640." In *The University in Society.* Vol. 1. Edited by Lawrence Stone. London: Oxford University Press, 1975.

Nash, Thomas. *Haue with you to Saffron-Walden; or, Gabriell Harueys Hunt is up etc.* London: John Danter, 1596.

Osgood, Charles Grosvenor. *Concordance to the Poems of Edmund Spenser.* Washington, DC: The Carnegie Institution of Washington, 1915.

————. "Spenser's English Rivers." *Transactions of the Connecticut Academy of Arts and Sciences* 23 (1920): 65–108.

Owen, Dorothy. *Cambridge University Archives: A Classified List.* Cambridge: Cambridge University Press, 1988.

Patterson, Annabel. *Pastoral and Ideology: Virgil to Valery.* Berkeley: University of California Press, 1987.

Paulson, Ronald. *The Literary Landscape: Turner and Constable.* New Haven: Yale University Press, 1982.

Piepho, Lee. "The Latin and English Eclogues of Phineas Fletcher: Sannazaro's *Piscatoria* among the Britons." *Studies in Philology* 81, no. 4 (1984): 461–72.

Poggioli, Renato. *The Oaten Flute: Essays on Pastoral Poetry and the Pastoral Ideal.* Cambridge: Harvard University Press, 1975.

Rosenberg, D. M. *Oaten Reeds and Trumpets: Pastoral and Epic in Virgil, Spenser, and Milton.* Lewisburg, PA: Bucknell University Press, 1981.

Rosenmeyer, Thomas G. *The Green Cabinet.* Berkeley: University of California Press, 1969.

Sannazaro, Jacopo. *Arcadia and Piscatorial Eclogues.* Translated by Ralph Nash. Detroit: Wayne State University Press, 1966.

Schleiner, Louise. "Spenser's 'E. K.' as Edmund Kent (Kenned/of Kent): Kyth (Couth), Kissed, and Kunning-Conning." *English Literary Renaissance* 20 (1990), 374–405.

Shakespeare, William. *The Complete Works.* Edited by Sylvan Barnet. New York: Harcourt, Brace Jovanovich, Inc., 1963.

Shore, David R. "Colin and Rosalind: Love and Poetry in the *Shepheardes Calender.*" *SP* 73 (1976): 176–88.

————. *Spenser and the Poetics of Pastoral.* Kingston: McGill-Queen's University Press, 1985.

Simon, Joan. *The Social Origins of English Education.* London: Student's Library of Education, 1970.

Smith, Gregory G. *Elizabethan Critical Essays.* Oxford: Clarendon Press, 1904.

Smith, Hallett. *Elizabethan Poetry: A Study in Conventions, Meaning, and Expression*. Cambridge: Harvard University Press, 1952.

Snell, Bruno. *The Discovery of the Mind: Greek Origins of European Thought*. Translated by T. G. Rosenmeyer. New York: Harper, 1960.

Snyder, Susan. *Pastoral Process: Spenser, Marvell, Milton*. Stanford: Stanford University Press, 1998.

Spenser, Edmund. *The Faerie Queene*. Edited by A. C. Hamilton. London: Longman, 1977.

———. *Poetical Works*. Edited by J. C. Smith and E. de Selincourt. New York: Oxford University Press, 1983.

———. *The Yale Edition of the Shorter Poems of Edmund Spenser*. Edited by William Orem et al. New Haven: Yale University Press, 1989.

Stewart, B. T. "A Borrowing from Spenser by Phineas Fletcher." *Modern Language Notes* 56 (1941): 273–74.

Tasso, Torquato. *Amintas: A Dramatick Pastoral*. Translated by William Ayre. London, 1737.

Tayler, Edward William. *Nature and Art in Renaissance Literature*. New York: Columbia University Press, 1964.

Tillyard, E. M. W. *Milton*. London: Chatto and Windus, 1930.

Toliver, Harold E. *Pastoral Forms and Attitudes*. Berkeley: University of California Press, 1971.

Tonkin, Humphrey. *Spenser's Courteous Pastoral: Book VI of "The Faerie Queene."* Oxford: Clarendon Press, 1972.

Twigg, John. *The University of Cambridge and the English Revolution, 1625–1688*. Cambridge: The Boydell Press, 1990.

Umstead, Radcliff Douglas. *The University World: A Synoptic View of Higher Education in the Middle Ages and The Renaissance*. Pittsburgh: Univ of Pittsburgh Publications in Medieval and Renaissance Studies, v. 2, 1973.

University Registry Guard Books in Cambridge University Archives: CUR: 2, 4, 6.1, 8, 11, 12, 13, 15, 16, 18, 20.1, 27, 78, 92.1, 93.

Varney, Anthony. "Milton's 'Uncouth Swain.' " *Notes and Queries* 29 (1982): 24–26.

Venn, John. *Early Collegiate Life*. Cambridge: W. Heffer and Sons n.p., 1913.

———. *Grace Book: Cambridge University Records, 1542–89*. Cambridge: Cambridge University Press, 1910.

Venn, John, and J. A. Venn. *Alumni Cantabrigienses*. Part 1. 4 vols. Cambridge: Cambridge University Press, 1922–1927.

Virgil. *Eclogues*. In *The Singer of the Eclogues: A Study of Virgilian Pastoral*. Translated by Paul Alpers. Berkeley: University of California Press, 1979.

Walton, Izaak. *The Compleat Angler; or, The Contemplative Man's Recreation. Being a Discourse of Fish and Fishing, Not Unworthy the Perusal of Most Anglers*. London: T. Maxey for R. Marriot, 1653.

Wedgwood, C. V. *Seventeenth Century English Literature*. London: Oxford University Press, 1970.

Williams, Kathleen. *Spenser's World of Glass*. Berkeley and Los Angeles: University of California Press, 1966.

Williams, Raymond. *The Country and the City*. New York: Oxford University Press, 1973.

Wind, Edgar. *Pagan Mysteries in the Renaissance*. Rev. ed. UK, New York: W.W. Norton, 1968.

Wittreich, Joseph. "From Pastoral to Prophesy: The Genres of 'Lycidas.' " *Milton Studies* 13 (1979): 59–80.

Wolfgang, Iser. "Spenser's Arcadia: The Interrelation of Fiction and History." In *Mimesis in Contemporary Theory*. Edited by Mihai Spariosu. Philadelphia: John Benjamins Publishing Company, 1984.

Index